HIDDEN HISTORY *of the* DARK CORNER

HIDDEN HISTORY
of the
DARK CORNER

Drew Hines

THE History PRESS

Published by The History Press
Charleston, SC
www.historypress.com

Unless otherwise noted, images are from the collection of the author.

First published 2024

Manufactured in the United States

ISBN 9781467156455

Library of Congress Control Number: 2023948359

Notice: The information in this book is true and complete to the best of our knowledge. It is offered without guarantee on the part of the author or The History Press. The author and The History Press disclaim all liability in connection with the use of this book.

This book is dedicated to the memory of two Dark Corner natives whose infectious love for the history and culture of this place they called home continues to teach and inspire those who come after them.

James A. Howard
(1894–1988)
Author of Dark Corner Heritage

Dean Stuart Campbell
(1934–2022)
The Squire of Dark Corner

CONTENTS

Contents

ACKNOWLEDGEMENTS

Jimmy Campbell
Carolyn Chisam
Geraldine Eppley
Darrell and Tonya Farmer
Natasha Hipp
Gavin Howard
Ralph Howard
Jimmy and Jagina Howard King
Hilda Howard Morrow
Charlie Wilson
Richard H. Wood
Alan Zordan

A special word of thanks to Candace Rathbone for her tireless work and expert assistance in preparing the manuscript for publication.

INTRODUCTION

At a Fourth of July celebration at Glassy Mountain Baptist Church in 1844, longtime Dark Corner resident Pleasant Barton offered the following toast: "The Dark Corner was a stigma thrown upon the people of the upper part of the district. May they, by their virtue and intelligence, raise a light that will expose and drive away ignorance and vice."[1]

Already this region had garnered an unseemly reputation among residents of other sections of Greenville County and beyond. Some of this may have well been deserved due to the mischief and mayhem that often took place up in those parts. Weekly reports in the Greenville papers told of the discovery of moonshine distilleries, as well as reports of murders committed there, most often connected with the illegal manufacture of blockade whiskey.

When talking about the so-called Dark Corner, two questions naturally come up. First, where exactly is the Dark Corner located? At one time, nobody wanted to admit they lived in the Dark Corner. Whenever curious strangers wandered up around Highland, or Glassy or Ebenezer, they would often ask a native, "Just where is the Dark Corner?" The suspicious resident would invariably reply, "Just a little further up the road." Because of this reluctance to positively identify the Dark Corner, there was naturally confusion about where it could be found. Nowadays there's wide agreement on its location. Most will now tell you the Dark Corner is basically the Glassy Mountain Township of Greenville County. The late Mann Batson and Dr. Jim Howard, author of *Dark Corner Heritage*, both hold this view.

The Glassy Mountain Township extends north just to the North Carolina line, reaching over the peaks of the two iconic Dark Corner landmarks, Hogback and Glassy Mountains. The southern border is South Carolina Highway 414, and the eastern border of the Dark Corner is the Spartanburg County line. To the west, US Highway 25 serves as the western border. So, within this well-defined geographical area lies the once elusive Dark Corner.

There is much less agreement about how the Dark Corner got its famous name. Evidently, considering Pleasant Barton's well-known and historic toast, the Dark Corner bore its name as early as 1844. Some believe it goes even further back to the days of the Nullification Crisis. The Nullification Crisis of 1832 threatened to tear the young United States of America apart thirty years before it happened. Even then there was widespread animosity between northerners and southerners over a variety of issues. Northern industrialists and politicians were bent on imposing a crippling tariff on imported foreign goods that would have had devastating consequences on the South, which had to import many of its manufactured goods, as it was basically an agrarian society. South Carolina's own John C. Calhoun led the fight against this action. The State of South Carolina was even threatening to secede from the Union and take military action if necessary. The intention was to "nullify" or basically ignore the tariff. It was a time of great uncertainty.

Residents of northern Greenville County, the independent-minded citizens that they were, were solidly opposed to nullification, and they most definitely were opposed to secession. Greenville resident and onetime governor of South Carolina Benjamin Perry claimed the Dark Corner earned its nickname during this period of great political unrest. He explained at a large public gathering held, once again, at Glassy Mountain Baptist Church:

> *I have said, fellow citizens, that this magnificent mountain country of yours was dubbed by the Nullifiers in 1832 the Dark Corner. A word of explanation for this sobriquet. There were two tickets for the legislature at that time before you. The one for nullification and the other for the American Union. The Nullification ticket, out of one hundred seventy votes polled at your precinct received one! Only one! This so maddened the Nullifiers that by way of reproach they termed Mason's Box the "Dark Corner" of Greenville County in which the light of Nullification could not shine.*

And yet the most widely accepted theory of how the Dark Corner got its name comes from still another tale of another political gathering that took place at the old muster ground up near South Carolina Highway 11. The muster ground was a popular public gathering spot and was the site of military drills and training exercises held by the old state militia, which was once very active in antebellum South Carolina. It was also here that area residents held barbecues, horse races and political rallies.

The story goes that at one political rally held at the muster ground around the time of the Civil War, a politician from Greenville was giving a political speech while standing in the back of a wagon so he could better be seen and heard. A couple of ruffians in the crowd evidently didn't agree with what the speaker was saying, so they picked up the shafts of the wagon and began rolling it. The speaker lost his balance and fell out of the wagon to the ground. No doubt the crowd roared with laughter as he stood to his feet and brushed off the dirt and dust. Embarrassed and humiliated, he announced, "You people up here are in the dark! You'll never see the light of day!" When he returned to Greenville and gave a report on what happened up in that dark corner of Greenville County, the name stuck. The Greenville papers famously picked on the Dark Corner and further promoted the name and the reputation that went with it.

Down through the years, the name Dark Corner has remained, and residents have borne it. In recent years, though, the Dark Corner name has become more celebrated than shunned. In fact, it has become a brand for many enterprising souls who have profited from the name. Legal moonshine, not manufactured in the hills but brewed in laboratory-like surroundings in Greenville, proudly bears the name "Dark Corner." T-shirts, hats, coffee mugs and other items are marketed using the Dark Corner name as well. Books, magazine articles and movies have been produced about this legendary locale. And so, it goes.

These days there may be few moonshine stills in the shadow of Hogback and Glassy, but the mystique and rich cultural heritage remain intact. And that is the essence of its hidden history. So many of the tales and anecdotes I share in this book are well known and have been often repeated. Longtime residents and those who have read the well-beloved books written over the years about the Dark Corner will recognize many of these stories I share.

Speaking of Dark Corner books, the fascination with Dark Corner lore and history really goes back to the 1980 publication of James A. Howard's classic *Dark Corner Heritage*. Howard, a retired Baptist minister, was eighty-six years of age when he sat down to chronicle this history. A Dark Corner native, he shared not only his vast resources of knowledge but also his great love for the place and people. *Dark Corner Heritage* became extremely popular and renewed a great interest in this storied region. Howard's assistant during this ambitious venture was a young forty-five-year-old advertising executive named Dean Stuart Campbell. Campbell was also a product of the Dark Corner, born and raised at the foot of Glassy Mountain. He assisted Dr. Howard in the design, artwork and publication of the landmark book. After Howard's death in 1988, Dean Campbell became the Dark Corner's leading expert and advocate. The late Jim McAlister, the popular human-interest columnist for the *Greenville News* during the 1970s and early '80s, created the title "Squire of Dark Corner" for Dean, who bore this title proudly up to the time of his death in 2022. Dean Campbell also wrote prolifically about the place he loved so well. And around 2017, he was commissioned to write a weekly column for the *Tryon Daily Bulletin* that he called "Twice Told Tales of the Dark Corner." From these weekly articles came two beloved books, compilations of his work for the Tryon paper. Dean's untimely passing in December 2022 has left a huge void in Dark Corner knowledge. He can simply never be replaced. I was honored to be his friend and cohort in much of the work he did in his latter days. We did lectures and conducted tours of the Dark Corner together, and I gleaned all the knowledge and wisdom I could from this fascinating and eloquent southern gentleman. Dean's last writing was the foreword he wrote for my book *North of Jordan*. And I remain deeply touched that he chose to do this for me.

And so, it is to the memory of Dr. James A. Howard and the Squire of Dark Corner, Dean Stuart Campbell, that I dedicate *Hidden History of the Dark Corner*.

And now I invite you to join me on this journey, as we travel "just a little further up the road."[2]

Drew Hines
2023

I

A TALE OF TWO BRIDGES

The Dark Corner of Greenville County has a more important and fascinating history associated with it than most people can imagine. For example, within its boundaries may be found both the oldest bridge in South Carolina (the Poinsett Bridge, built in 1820) and the last remaining wooden covered bridge in South Carolina (the Campbell Covered Bridge, constructed in 1909). Both bridges, though no longer in use, serve as landmarks of the picturesque Dark Corner.

THE POINSETT BRIDGE

From the earliest days of permanent settlement in the upstate of South Carolina, western North Carolina and even beyond, people pondered the possibility of building a road across the hills and valleys on which marketable goods could be transported to Charleston, Savannah and Augusta. Early frontier roads were narrow and barely passable, especially during certain times of the year. Most originated as ancient Indian warrior paths or even animal trails. Enterprising souls dreamed of the day when Tennessee, Kentucky and western North Carolina farmers could easily transport their crops and herds to the market. From this early and ambitious dream would emerge what would come to be known as the State Road.

The Poinsett Bridge, built in 1820.

In 1818, a group of prominent South Carolinians organized a committee to closely examine the possibilities of constructing this statewide road. This first board consisted of five members and included the well-known South Carolinian Joel Roberts Poinsett. Poinsett, born in Charleston in 1779 to an aristocratic French Huguenot family, grew up in a home that encouraged education and public service. After representing South Carolina in the U.S. House of Representatives, Poinsett went on to become the American minister to Mexico and later served as secretary of war under President Martin Van Buren. Of course, most people remember the name Joel Poinsett because while serving in Mexico he cultivated a beautiful red tropical flower that was later named poinsettia in his honor. Few people are aware, however, of the critical role Poinsett played in establishing a statewide series of roads and canals.

Colonel Abram Blanding is less well known than Poinsett, yet he too played an active role in the creation of the State Road. Born in Massachusetts in 1775, Blanding later moved to South Carolina, first to Camden and then to Columbia, where, among other things, he practiced law and became the first principal of the Columbia Male Academy. Abram Blanding, like Joel Poinsett, was a visionary leader and philanthropist.

When the State of South Carolina created a Board of Public Works in 1817 to oversee the development of a statewide road and canal system, both Poinsett and Blanding seemed to be natural choices to serve on the five-man board. In 1822, Blanding was tapped to serve as superintendent of public works, and he maintained that position until 1827.[3]

One of the very first projects of the newly created Board of Public Works was to create a State Road that would traverse South Carolina, extending from Charleston in the east all the way to the upper reaches of the South Carolina mountains in the west. Naturally, construction in the lower part of the state was much simpler and proceeded rapidly because of the flat terrain of the Lowcountry and the Midlands. The problems came above the Fall Line, where engineers and laborers had to negotiate hills, hollers, creeks, rivers and mountains. Joel Poinsett was appointed to supervise the difficult task of roadbuilding through the mountains above Traveler's Rest. Construction commenced in earnest after the Blanding and Poinsett appointments in 1818. According to local lore passed down through the years, Poinsett took up residence in the former home of Colonel Wilson Barton up off current-day US Highway 25.[4]

The labor force on the State Road consisted of locals, along with some enslaved labor. The skilled stonemasons who crafted bridges and culverts

Stone culvert from the State Road, 1820. *Courtesy of Jimmy Pruitt.*

were, for the most part, brought into the area from the Northeast through recruitment and newspaper solicitation. Many of these craftsmen were Irish immigrants eager for adventure and opportunity on the new frontier. These stonemasons were responsible for building the rock walls that acted as truss supports for the winding roadbeds, offering stability and curbing erosion. They also laid the stonework for some forty-four culverts placed along the way, as well as the three major bridges that spanned rivers and creeks.

During the construction of this mountain section of the State Road, many of the workers became desperately ill as a result of a persistent fever that raged in the work camps.[5] These outbreaks seriously delayed road construction. Attrition among the workers was a real problem as well. Still, work continued despite the difficulties and was finally completed in the autumn of 1820.

The bridges on this stretch of the State Road must have all been wonders to behold. The bridge over the Saluda River featured two Gothic arches fifteen feet wide. The bridge was 60 feet long and 15 feet high. It collapsed several years ago. Another one of Poinsett's bridges spanned Hodge's Creek and was smaller than the Saluda River bridge. It was 12.5 feet high and featured one circular arch. This bridge disappeared under the waters of the Greenville Reservoir when the land was flooded in 1958.[6] The one remaining bridge (there are also some culverts and retaining walls still standing) is now known as the Poinsett Bridge, and it spans Gap Creek. The beautifully crafted structure boasts an impressive 15-foot-high Gothic arch, complete with a keystone at its apex. It's 7 feet wide to accommodate the heavy foot and wagon traffic it saw back in the day. The bridge extends 130 feet from one end to the other. One can now only imagine the beauty and the intricacy of the other two "Poinsett" bridges that were built along the way and are now long extinct.

Today's visitors can enjoy the lovely historic Poinsett Bridge because it is currently a protected site. A twenty-first-century visitor to this place can only imagine what a feat of engineering the construction of this bridge must have been. As you stand on the bridge, you can almost envision the steady stream of hogs, horses, cattle, mules and turkeys crossing the Poinsett from all points west and what a job it must have been driving these animals all the way to the coastal cities beyond. It was a grueling journey that would have taken weeks—it's been estimated that these slow-moving animal caravans moved only about eight miles a day.

Of course, down through the years, legends, tales and ghost stories about the bridge have frequently popped up. Most of them originated around campfires at the nearby Boy Scout camp called Camp Old Indian. Many of these spectral fables were woven around the legends of the sick and dying laborers who worked on the road and bridge. Usually, they told of a worker who died on the job and was hastily buried inside of the unfinished bridge or simply placed in a shallow grave close by. None of these makeshift burials can be documented, but a tale about a phantom Irish stonemason roaming along the Poinsett Bridge in the darkness of night would certainly send chills up the spine of any tenderfoot Scout, and sleep would not come easily!

Another lesser-known ghost tale about the environs of the Poinsett Bridge involves the story of a girl escaping slavery who was caught by her master on the bridge and, as punishment, was hacked to death with an axe. Again, this story, like the others, would be hard to prove and is most likely just a fantasy, but it so perfectly adds to the mystique of this magical place where one feels like a time traveler, keenly connected to the past.[7]

The Campbell Covered Bridge

Covered bridges are a part of Americana that call up images of clear streams and verdant pastures along with quaint lithographs by Currier and Ives. These unique structures made their first appearance in Connecticut back in 1804 with a bridge spanning the Hudson River. Their popularity grew from there, and for generations these beautiful and useful covered bridges were constructed all across America. They served their purpose well, but because they were composed primarily of wood, their lifespans were considerably reduced due to the constant stress of passing traffic and the natural process of deterioration that lumber undergoes over time. Of course, they were also subject to vandalism and even arson. And because of all this, when they were no longer able to be used, they were most often replaced by more modern steel structures.

Today it is estimated that only about seven hundred covered bridges remain in the United States, and most of them see little if any traffic because of age and condition. The last remaining covered bridge in South Carolina can be found in the heart of the Dark Corner. Commonly known as the Campbell Covered Bridge, this beautiful old local landmark was built in 1909 to span Beaverdam Creek. It has a long, rich and celebrated history.

The Campbell Covered Bridge, built in 1909.

The bridge was named for local resident Alexander Lafayette Campbell (1836–1920), who owned the property adjacent to the fabled structure. He also operated a gristmill close by. Campbell was a much-respected member of the Dark Corner community. A Confederate veteran who had also been a prisoner of war, Campbell fathered a large family of children, and many of his descendants are still in the area. He is buried in the cemetery of Ebenezer-Welcome Baptist Church.

Back in the day, the Campbell Covered Bridge saw quite a bit of traffic come across its covered timbers, being located on a busy country road from Gowensville to Pleasant Hill. The bridge also accommodated motor traffic until it was finally closed off to all traffic in the early 1980s. Berms were situated at both entrances of the old bridge so no cars could pass through.

The bridge was designed and built by local contractor Charles Irwin Willis. Construction began in 1909. The bridge is thirty-eight feet long, twelve feet wide, and constructed mainly of heavy pine beams.[8]

Attempts to save the bridge began in 1964 when the Crescent Garden Club of Greenville funded some limited restoration efforts. More renovation work was done in 1990, and then finally the Greenville County Recreation District purchased the property in 2009, ensuring that the Campbell Covered Bridge would be preserved for future generations and remain a favorite Dark Corner destination.

Both the Poinsett Bridge and the Campbell Covered Bridge stand the test of time, thanks to the careful intervention of county residents who recognize their historic as well as nostalgic value. They both harken back to a much simpler and slower way of life. As you stand inside the Campbell Covered Bridge, you can almost hear the *clip-clop* of horse hooves as they pass through the cool darkness of the bridge. Or perhaps it's the rhythmic swooshing of the wheel of Fate Campbell's mill that you hear as it breaks through the waters of Beaverdam Creek. Whatever image the old bridge brings to mind, it makes you glad that this beautiful landmark of the Dark Corner is still standing.

2

ON TOP OF OLD HOGBACK

Besides the two iconic bridges in the Dark Corner, many folks would associate this lovely region with the majestic mountains that serve as a dramatic backdrop for it. In particular, most tend to think of Hogback and Glassy.

Glassy Mountain, just west of Hogback, is easily identifiable with its breathtakingly beautiful sheer rock face. For several years, adventurous souls tempted fate by sailing off Glassy's 2,776-foot peak on hang gliders. Spectators in a grassy meadow below would hold their breath until the quiet winged gliders safely and silently touched the ground. The Dark Corner's Glassy Mountain (to be distinguished from a peak over in Pickens County with the same name) is perhaps the better known of the two because of the Cliffs at Glassy, a world-class golfing community situated high atop its summit. Completed in 1993, the Cliffs was the dream of the enterprising Greenville real estate developer Jim Anthony. When a person recalls what the top of Glassy Mountain looked like prior to the Cliffs Community, one can truly appreciate the vision and foresight it took to see the possibility of a development like this on top of a mountain that was virtually inaccessible and little more than a stony knob covered with third- and fourth-growth timber, tangled vines and rattlesnakes. Glassy had been a well-known lair for moonshiners for generations. There were a few families who still lived close by, like the famous Plumley sisters. But for the most part, Glassy was abandoned during World War I when an artillery range was entrenched at the bottom of the mountain, and families were moved off so that soldiers from Camp Wadsworth in Spartanburg could take target practice at the mountain with their heavy artillery.

Anthony and his ambitious partners went to work purchasing the land, which was mostly divided into small tracts that had been bought and sold over the years. Getting clear titles and deeds on some of this real estate was a real headache for Cliffs at Glassy lawyers. Once the land was legally purchased and the myriad permits obtained, Anthony and his partners secured the services of well-known golf architect Tom Jackson, whose creativity would truly be put to the test on the top of Glassy Mountain. Jackson had spent most of his professional life designing prize-winning coastal courses. Now he was tasked with the awesome responsibility of designing a mountain course of great distinction. And he accomplished that and much more. These days, you may not see the hang gliders of yesteryear sailing off the top of Glassy, but if you look closely, you'll see a stunning little chapel that appears to be merely clinging to the edge of the summit. A popular wedding venue, the chapel serves as a reminder that a new era has arrived on Glassy Mountain. Moonshiners have been replaced by millionaires who are trying their luck on one of the most beautiful and challenging mountain golf courses in America.

One of the few reminders of the old days on Glassy is the venerable Mountain Hill Baptist Church. The site of an infamous nineteenth-century shootout, which is the subject of another chapter in this book, a beautiful new building has been erected where modern worshipers, some of whom live in the Cliffs community, can come and pay homage to the One Who put the mountain there in the first place.

The Dark Corner's other highly visible and legendary peak is Hogback Mountain, so-called because the mountain and surrounding hills, from a distance, resemble the back of a hog in a prone position. Hogback Mountain is especially prominent on the northern horizon because, of course, of its superior height, which dwarfs other peaks around it. The summit of Hogback is at 3,240 feet, almost 1,000 feet higher than its more diminutive neighbor Glassy Mountain. It can easily be spotted for miles. At night it is especially visible because of the flashing red beacon high atop its apex. This constantly flashing light marks the spot for the transmitter of WSPA-TV 7 in Spartanburg, and it's been in this strategic location since 1963, when broadcasting pioneer and mogul Walter Brown secured long-term leases on the mountainous real estate. Because of Channel Seven's lease, along with the fact that much of the Hogback property is in the hands of the Greenville Water System, the mountain is mostly inaccessible to the public today.

The rich, long history of Hogback Mountain is carefully chronicled in a book written by James Stehlik in 2011, *Distilling the Mysteries of Hogback Mountain*. This well-researched volume is a thorough, painstaking study of the history and mystery of this great mountain. And it is recommended for those who want to do a more careful study of this subject.

The amazing story of Hogback Mountain goes far back before the misty memories of men, even to a time in the far distant past before the Cherokee populated the land. A series of petroglyphs (early human designs carved into rocks) can be found along the sides of Hogback, and what a treasure they are. The fact that few people are allowed on the mountain has probably

View of Glassy Mountain. *Photo from* Eyes to the Hills, *by Dean Campbell. Used by permission.*

ensured their preservation over the years. They have been kept safe from vandalism, but at the same time, it's a shame more people can't behold their beautiful and intricate artistry. These may very well be of Cherokee design, but many researchers think they even predate the Cherokee. And of course, there's no doubt the Cherokee did inhabit this land before the Europeans arrived. Indian artifacts are plentiful on and around the mountain, even as they are across the whole Dark Corner.

Early settlers to the region, for the most part, arrived after the American Revolution, but there were also some hardy adventurers who had moved in

Native American relics found in the Dark Corner.

well before the war. One of the most feared and despised characters of this era was the murderous Loyalist marauder Bloody Bill Bates, who maintained his den of thieves in a lost cove near the foot of Hogback Mountain. From there he launched his cruel, bloodthirsty attacks on Patriot families, robbing, raping and murdering in monstrous fashion. Undoubtedly, his most infamous raid took place at old Fort Gowen, located on the much-traveled Blackstock Road just south of Landrum, in September 1781. A band of Patriots, fearing a Loyalist rampage, were holed up in Fort Gowen, prepared to defend themselves. This group included not only men but women and children as well. Bates and his Tory raiders greatly outnumbered the occupants of the fort. A siege was planned, but first, Bates falsely offered clemency to the group should they surrender immediately. Once Bates was given access to the fort, he and his desperados ruthlessly murdered men, women and children. Those who were able to escape ran for help, but it was too late. However, in the long run, justice was carried out on the cruel Loyalist leader. After the war, Bates was arrested in Polk County, North Carolina, for horse stealing, and he was carried to Greenville, South Carolina, to stand trial. Enter John Motley. Motley's family had been attacked by Bates in June 1781 near Motlow Creek in Spartanburg County. John watched as his family was bludgeoned, shot and tomahawked to death. He escaped but, of course, never forgot that day—nor did he forget Bloody Bill Bates. When word reached John Motley over in Spartanburg County that Bates had finally been apprehended and jailed, he grabbed his pistol and collected some friends together to travel to Greenville. When they arrived, they demanded the jail keys from the surprised and greatly outnumbered jailor. He complied, and Motley pulled Bates from his cell, took him outside and shot him to death. A shallow grave was hastily dug, and the body of the former murderer was unceremoniously tossed in it. Bates still lies today in a forgotten, unmarked grave somewhere in downtown Greenville. Thus, Bloody Bill Bates died as he lived—violently.

After the American Revolution, the young government, strapped for cash, paid veterans of the war with land grants to tracts in the western part of the state, just claimed from the Cherokee. One of the area's first pioneer settlers to be given land on Hogback was Robert Goodgion, who received his land grant for 186 acres on the crest of Hogback Mountain on January 2, 1811.[9] The Goodgion family gave its name to Goodjoin Road in the upper part of Greenville County, with a slight variation on the spelling of the name. Others followed the Goodgions into the Dark Corner—intrepid souls all—who braved the wild and wrested a living from the thin, rocky soil.

It wasn't long before many of the subsistence farmers on and around Hogback learned that distilled corn demanded a much higher price than corn sold by the bushel. It was then that the war between the United States government and the private unlicensed distiller really began. And this was a war that, on occasion, became brutal and bloody, as it was fought with shotguns, pistols and Winchester rifles. Some of the epic battles of this war are detailed in other parts of this book.

The twentieth century arrived on Hogback Mountain with little fanfare, but the new century would bring with it many unprecedented events and people to its idyllic surroundings. There is, for example, the story of a famous picnic that took place high atop Hogback somewhere around 1918. The story goes that Henry Ford, Thomas Edison and Harvey Firestone, three titans of American industry in the early twentieth century, were vacationing together, as they often did, at Dr. Edwin Wiley Grove's famous Grove Park Inn in Asheville, North Carolina. This renowned trio spent many summers together, along with, at various times, famed American naturalist John Burroughs and oil tycoon John D. Rockefeller. They called themselves the "Vagabonds," and no one knew where they would show up next during their summer outings together. The excuse they frequently offered for their travels was that they were road testing Ford automobiles and Firestone tires on the rocky dirt backroads of rural America.

Allegedly, the famed trio started out one bright summer morning from Asheville and drove across the mountains to the quaint, charming, toy-making village of Tryon. They then proceeded out of Tryon onto the Rocky Spur Road that led to the summit of Hogback Mountain, where they enjoyed a delicious picnic lunch that had been packed for them at the Grove Park Inn. After lunching together and enjoying the rugged scenery and the breathtaking view, they packed up and returned to the "Land of the Sky."

The problem with this story is that both Hogback and Glassy Mountains were still under lease to the federal government in 1918 as an artillery range for training soldiers from Spartanburg's Camp Wadsworth. And the land was not released back to the original owners until 1919. Granted, artillery fire ceased there in April 1918, but the question would be, was the Rocky Spur Road indeed open for public travel during the summer of 1918? No doubt, the now famous outing could have taken place the following year, or even the next, but we do know for a fact that the Vagabonds were in Asheville in 1918. It's fascinating to speculate about this Hogback visit by these American superstars, and one must wonder what they would have thought of our beautiful Dark Corner scenery.

THE ILL-FATED BLUE RIDGE FOREST

Most people don't know that the Cliffs at Glassy was not the first mountaintop golf community in the Dark Corner. Not by a long shot!

In the early 1920s, the world was flocking to the mountains of western North Carolina. In the late nineteenth century, the arrival of the railroad to Asheville opened all kinds of opportunities and possibilities for the charming mountain village. Multimillionaire George Washington Vanderbilt, while vacationing in the Land of the Sky, decided this garden spot, with its limitless mountain vistas, would be the perfect place to build the largest, most lavish private residence in America. And he spared no cost in doing it. Several thousand acres of unspoiled mountain and valley land were purchased by the New York industrialist. And Vanderbilt didn't just stop with building an opulent castle. He built an entire village, complete with an awe-inspiring church, to surround the Biltmore House. Others followed. The Grove Park Inn came along and became a world-class hotel, and thus, Asheville became the playground of the rich and famous. Its charm, not to mention its temperate mountain climate, attracted people from everywhere. In fact, it was that temperate mountain climate and fresh, clean air that was believed to have healing properties that could possibly even cure the dreaded killer of that day: tuberculosis. And so, sanitariums were now dotting the hillsides around the once sleepy mountain village.

As a result of all this, there was a land boom of sorts that extended all the way from Asheville through the North Carolina mountains and foothills. And this boom soon made its way to the charming little mountain hamlet of Tryon, well known already for its cottage toy-making industry.

So, building on this movement, in 1924 a consortium of northern businessmen began buying up timber rights and land options and making real estate purchases outright, including close to two hundred acres on and around Hogback Mountain, just south of Tryon. They formed Hogback Mountain Inc., which was the chief developing arm of Blue Ridge Forest of the Carolina Mountains.[10] The intention of this development group was to create a world-class golfing community high atop Hogback. Lots would be sold to potential residents, and the hope was that this community would grow and attract others to the mountain. After all, the Roaring Twenties were times of unlimited optimism and big dreams. Fortunes were made, and they soon would be lost.

A lovely community clubhouse was soon raised, its rustic construction reflecting the rugged terrain around it, built of native stone and sturdy American chestnut. A large Olympic-sized swimming pool would be a haven for weary golfers after an invigorating round. This pool was spring fed and always contained plenty of the cold mountain water that people seemed to love so much.

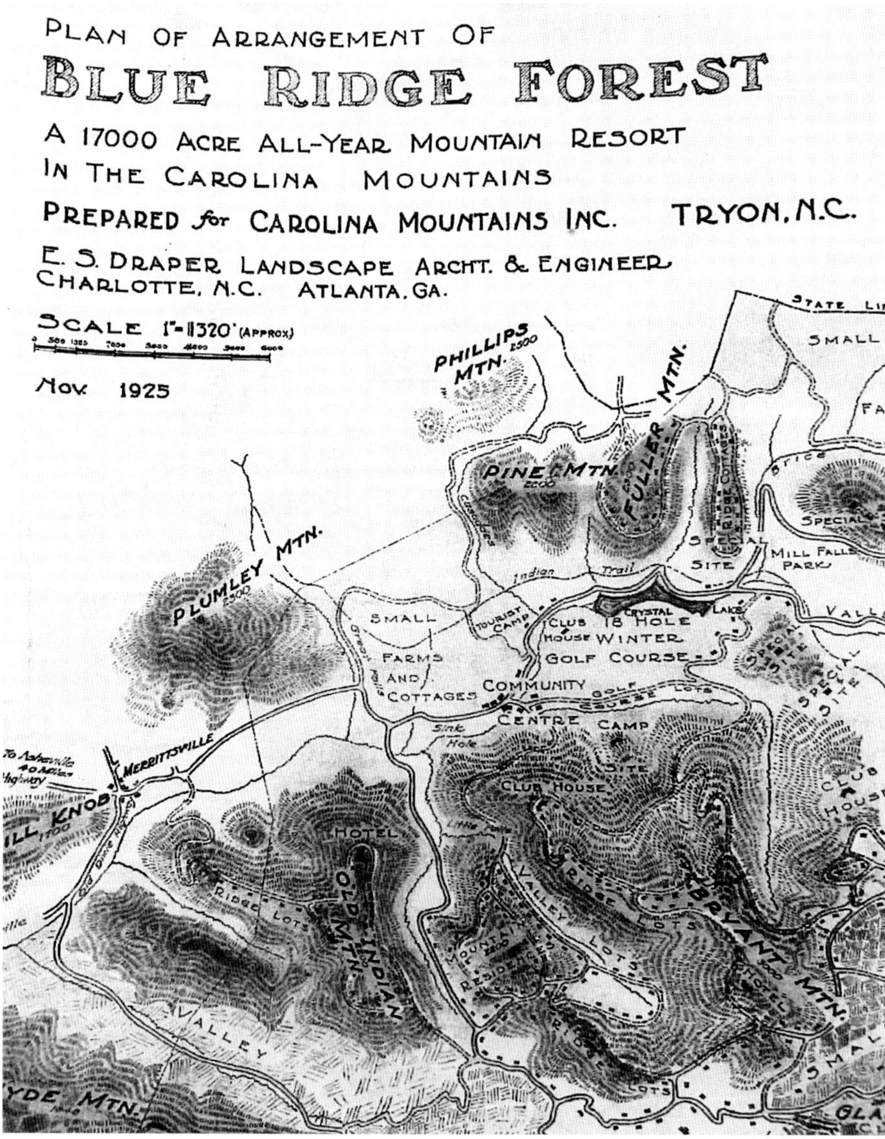

A 1925 map of the Blue Ridge Forest. *Courtesy of Charlie Wilson.*

But of course, the crown jewel of the Blue Ridge Forest was the masterfully designed and perfectly manicured golf course that was situated on a tabletop plateau of the mountain. The world-renowned golf architect Devereux Emmet was engaged to submit a design for this idyllic setting. Emmet had earned his reputation as one of the world's top golf course designers with beautiful and challenging courses like the

Chimney from Blue Ridge Forest, cabin 1.

Above: Publicity photo of Blue Ridge Forest swimming pool. *Courtesy of Charlie Wilson.*

Opposite: Chimney from Blue Ridge Forest, cabin 2.

Garden City Golf Club in Garden City, New York, as well as the world-famous Congressional Course in Bethesda, Maryland.

Roads to accommodate the expected high volume of traffic were cut to the top of Hogback. Advertisements for Blue Ridge Forest appeared

in many of the major newspapers of America. Yet in spite all these noble efforts, the sales of lots were disappointing.[11] Investors, though, continued to pour money into the seemingly doomed project. And then to seal that doom, the stock market crashed in October 1929. Blue Ridge Forest, strapped for much needed cash, would soon die a slow, painful death.

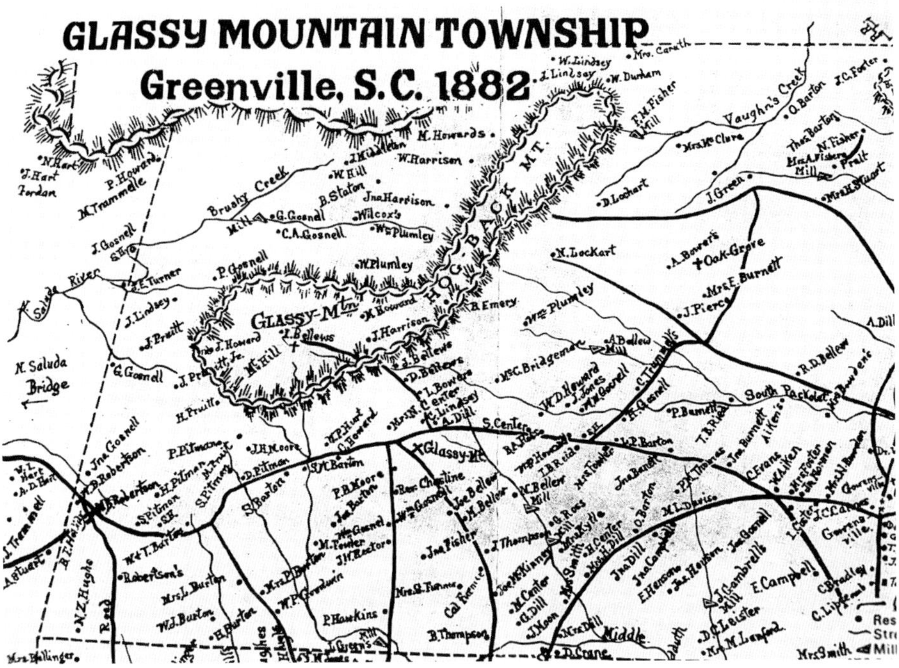

Glassy Mountain Township from the 1882 Kyzer map.

One of Blue Ridge Forest's chief investors and developers, R.C. Remick, was killed in an automobile accident a few years later in July 1935.

Today, all that remains of this once promising venture are the rocky shells of cabins, clubhouses and outbuildings. Visitors can still see the remnants of the cement pool, long taken over by vines and trees. Because traffic on top of Hogback has been so limited by WSPA-TV and the Greenville Water System, some relics of the Dark Corner's first luxury golfing community remain. And these remains are ghostly reminders that the best laid plans of men are subject to demise by circumstances beyond their control. And yet, the majestic mountain itself remains for all time, and its beauty endures, reminding all of the inspiring words of the Psalmist, who said in Psalm 121:

> *I will lift up mine eyes unto the hills from which cometh my help? My help cometh from the LORD, which made heaven and earth.*

3

A STORY OF TRUE FRIENDSHIP

On the frontier in colonial America, relations between white settlers and their Native American neighbors were often characterized by enmity and open hostility. One party would customarily initiate a bloody raid on the other, followed by a similar act of violence from the other side, often bloodier and more brutal than the first. There were rare exceptions to this rule. Sometimes history tells the story of tender friendships that developed between individuals from these two groups of sworn enemies. Everyone, of course, is familiar with the tale of the true friendship between Pocahontas and Captain John Smith in early Jamestown. Then we read of how Squanto of New England's Patuxet tribe befriended the Pilgrims and helped them to survive their first brutal winter in Massachusetts. And much later, history records the important contact the Lewis and Clark expedition made with a Shoshone woman named Sacagawea. Had it not been for her careful guidance and direction, the success of the expedition would have been in doubt. Not so familiar, though, is the story of a friendship that developed between Dark Corner pioneer and patriot Thomas Howard and a young Cherokee man named Skyuka.

The year 1776 was a dangerous and perilous time on the frontier of western South Carolina. It was not only a time of political revolution in the young colonies, but it was also a period of unprecedented unrest and hostility among the Cherokee. In 1755, South Carolina's Royal Governor James Glen met with representatives of the Cherokee Nation, led by their Chief Old Hop. A tenuous treaty was hammered out between representatives of both the state and the Cherokee peoples. Known as Glen's Treaty, this pact basically recognized the sovereign rule of England's king over all territory in the state, but as a tip of the hat to the Native Americans, the treaty ceded all lands west of the current day Greenville County line to the Cherokee.

As time went on, white settlers continued to push farther into Indian territory, testing the patience of the already frustrated Cherokee. In the meantime, representatives of the British government who were living among the Cherokee were doing all they could to inflame the resentment of the Indians toward the whites. This would prove to be a brilliant strategy: it would essentially distract the colonists from their revolutionary activities, since they would have to fight a war on two fronts. And the British weren't just encouraging the Cherokee to attack white settlements; they were also equipping them to do so.

This is where young Thomas Howard comes to prominence. Little is known about this intrepid youth other than the fact that he was, at the time, a Dark Corner resident, residing near present-day Tigerville. By all accounts, Howard was a captain in the local militia, which would certainly be unusual for a youth of sixteen. This has led to speculation that either his birthdate, which is commonly recorded as 1760, is wrong or that his rank was, in fact, sergeant or lieutenant. So, obviously there appear to be some problems with the facts of this account, but be that as it may, I will present the story as it has been reported for generations.

One day young Thomas Howard was turkey hunting in the vicinity of modern-day Tryon. He came across a young Cherokee warrior who had been bitten by a rattlesnake. Howard threw down his rifle and immediately went to work trying to save the young Indian's life, lancing the area of the snake bite with his hunting knife and sucking out the deadly venom. Thus, he saved the stranger's life. The youthful Cherokee introduced himself to his newfound friend as Skyuka, a Cherokee word for "chipmunk." The two young men from such diverse backgrounds became fast friends. We can assume they may have spent much time together afterward—although, we can only speculate about that.

What we do know is that in the spring of 1776, tensions between white settlers and the Cherokee grew to fever pitch. No one on the frontier at that time really felt safe. As a result, a network of crude forts was hastily erected along the Cherokee line. These included Fort Gowen, just south of modern-day Landrum on the old Blackstock Road; Earle's Fort, north of Landrum; Wood's Fort, near current-day Apalache; and Fort Prince, close to what we now know as Wellford. These primitive structures provided some measure of protection for the vulnerable settlers, who were constantly bracing themselves for Indian attacks.

Site of the original Block House.

Much earlier, in 1752, the famous Block House near Tryon, North Carolina, was constructed to offer protection for pioneer settlers there. It was here, probably close to the end of May 1776, that young Skyuka came to find Captain Howard. Skyuka had information that his Cherokee brothers were planning an attack on the Block House, and he wanted to warn his friend who had saved his life.

Together they devised a brilliant plan to preempt the Indian offensive. The Cherokee were gathered on nearby Round Mountain, a 2,418-foot peak in Polk County, North Carolina. The Indians, along with their Loyalist allies, were planning their strategy.

There existed a little-known gap in the mountain that had a winding trail. There was no way the Cherokee could have guessed that their white attackers would have known about this rear approach. Howard hastily gathered a group of fighters who met at the Block House and planned their attack. That evening, under the cover of darkness, they proceeded to the foot of Round Mountain, toward the Cherokee front. There they built a series of decoy bonfires, resembling campfires, and suggesting a campsite for the would-be attackers. A handful of soldiers were left behind to make this campsite look occupied. At the same time, Howard and the rest of his corps, led by the valiant Skyuka, proceeded through the gap of the mountains toward the unguarded rear of the Indians. Immediately, the Patriots began firing volleys into the warriors' camp, surprising the Indians and causing a general state of confusion among them, leading to great calamity. The assault was a total surprise. The battle was brief and deadly, and Captain Howard and his men prevailed, returning to the Block House victoriously.[12] The date, according to all tradition, was June 1, 1776.

After the Indian depredations ceased and the American Revolution ended, Captain Thomas Howard returned to the life of a Dark Corner farmer, raising a large family of children. And most modern-day Howards in the upstate can trace their lineage directly to the hero of Round Mountain.

Gravestone of Captain Thomas Howard. *Courtesy of Ralph Howard.*

Much less is known about the fate of young Skyuka. The story goes that he was later captured by the Cherokee and was tortured and then hanged from a sycamore tree for the crime of treason against his people. A mountain and a stream in Polk County have been named in honor of him, and the town of Tryon and the county of Polk were almost named for him. For whatever reason, that never materialized, to the chagrin of many who wished there were memorials to the young brave Cherokee warrior who paid the price for his loyalty and friendship. The gap through which he led Howard and his soldiers was later named Howard's Gap in honor of Thomas Howard. An early road that passed through the gap from near Spartanburg, South Carolina, all the way to Asheville, North Carolina, is named Howard Gap Road. In 1964, a large stone monument was erected commemorating Captain Howard's victory. It was later moved to a hillside just off I-26, and then it was moved once again to the city of Columbus, North Carolina, where it can be viewed today.

Thomas Howard lived to the ripe old age of seventy-eight, dying at his home, surrounded by his family in 1838. And thus ends the story of two young men thrust into the spotlight by history and the friendship they forged during dark and dangerous times.

4
A MOUNTAIN BOY'S LIFE STORY

The title of this chapter is taken from the title of an early autobiography of the late J. Dean Crain. This book is considered by many to be the first written record of what life was really like in the Dark Corner in the late nineteenth and early twentieth centuries, and though long out of print, old copies may be found occasionally online. The book is a real treasure. Dean Crain was one of the most prominent and influential individuals to come out of the Dark Corner and was, no doubt, one of the Dark Corner's favorite sons. And best of all, he was proud of his heritage and spoke of it often.

John Dean Crain was born on October 25, 1881, as the fifth of seven children born to David Hoke and Jane Suddeth Crain. The Crain family had settled in the Dark Corner a generation or two before Dean's birth. They were subsistence farmers, poor but proud. And like so many of their neighbors, the Crains distilled illegal corn whiskey. This was most certainly an economic consideration for the Crains and many others because corn, the main Dark Corner crop, sold so much better by the gallon than it did the bushel.

In *A Mountain Boy's Life Story*, Dean described the practice of making whiskey like this: "As I have said, it was the custom of the people to make whiskey. They thought they had the right to make it, and when I became large enough to know anything, I thought my life work was making whiskey."[13]

So, this was the backdrop of Dean Crain's early life. He and his younger brother Beaufort (I have noticed variations on the spelling of this name, but this is the spelling used on his grave marker, so this is the one I will use), who was also destined for the ministry, not only took up the practice of making blockade whiskey but also, early on, developed a taste for it. Later, of course, the great Baptist preacher and statesman Dean Crain would spend his life renouncing the use and the manufacture of strong drink. Again, in *A Mountain Boy's Life Story*, he wrote, "There is nothing that so completely destroys the whole man as does the habit of drink."[14] For Dean it was a circuitous journey that took him from making and drinking alcohol to declaring war on it. And for him this journey would begin at the age of seventeen.

North Greenville Academy (now North Greenville University) was an academic institution that sprang up in the Dark Corner community of Tigerville in 1891. Its founding was the result of a strong desire among North Greenville Association Baptists to bring educational opportunity to an area that was greatly in need. With the closing of Gowensville's Earle Seminary in 1889, on the death of its founder, Reverend Thomas J. Earle, there was an immediate void of educational opportunity for Dark Corner youth. So, North Greenville Academy came about as an attempt to help fill this void. The school offered a basic high school curriculum.

At the encouragement of family and friends who saw much potential in him, J. Dean Crain became a full-time student at the academy, making the daily five-mile journey from his parents' house on foot. Almost immediately, there was a noticeable and dramatic change in the young man's life. Not only was he exposed to a wealth of knowledge he had never known, but even more importantly, he also was exposed to a degree of Christian influence that was largely foreign to him at that point in his life. The effect on the young man was powerful. First, there was the challenge that he offered his brother Beaufort that they quit drinking moonshine for a time. Initially, the challenge was but for a few months, but then the ban on alcohol became permanent and lifelong. Both young men had seen firsthand the toll that alcohol was taking on the lives of their friends and family and realized that no good could come from it. And then, in a summertime revival meeting at Ebenezer-Welcome Baptist Church, Dean Crain experienced a true Christian conversion, and his experience was authentic, powerful and life-changing.

When Dean returned for his next term at North Greenville, he was a changed man. He seemed to have a new purpose and a new direction in life. This transformation was noticed by all. He would soon enter Furman University. It was while at Furman that Dean encountered many new experiences, some humorous, and he recounts many of them in his 1914 book. And it was here at Furman that Dean really began feeling he had been called to the gospel ministry. And this call was further confirmed when he went on to enter Richmond College in Richmond, Virginia. In Richmond, the boy from the Dark Corner was given his very first opportunity to preach in church. He chose the subject of Jonah as his first sermon topic. By his own admission, he said his first attempt at preaching was shaky at best. As time went on, his oratorical skills improved dramatically. In fact, while at Richmond, he won the school's medal for preaching.

In an interesting turn of events, in 1910, Dean Crain was invited to become the principal of his alma mater, North Greenville Academy. Crain's time there was notable and productive. It was during his tenure at North Greenville that Dean Crain discovered he had an uncanny ability to raise money, a gift that would serve him well in the years ahead as a builder of churches and, later, as a trustee of Furman University. Crain oversaw some significant physical improvements to the school during his brief two-year tenure. There were also some noticeable improvements in general student behavior and morale as well as a great spiritual fervor among the people, both students and faculty.

On June 10, 1908, Dean Crain's life further changed forever when he married Ellen Wilson, whom he had known and adored for a number of years. Their forty-seven-year marriage was a partnership of love and dedicated service to the Kingdom of God.

Meanwhile, J. Dean Crain was becoming well known among the Baptists of South Carolina, who recognized him as a man of impeccable character and integrity. His effectiveness as a pastor was being carefully observed during his tenure at City View Baptist Church in Greenville and then Park Street Baptist Church in Columbia. It was in 1928, while at Park Street, that South Carolina Baptists elected the boy from the Dark Corner to the prestigious position of president of the South Carolina Baptist Convention. He was also soon elected to his first term as a trustee of Furman University. He would go on to serve several more terms on this board during his long and illustrious career.

Without a doubt, Crain's most productive years of ministry would be as pastor of the Pendleton Street Baptist Church in Greenville, where he would serve with distinction for twenty-one years, from 1931 to 1952. The church grew greatly during his time there. While pastor at Pendleton Street, a large sanctuary was built to accommodate the many people who

Reverend J. Dean Crain. *From the* Tryon Daily Bulletin, *"Moonshiner Turned Preacher," Tuesday, July 24, 2012.*

were coming week in and week out to hear the great preacher, who was known for his folksy flair and humor in his preaching but was also well known for the unforgettable points he made in his sermons and the powerful conclusions they came to. Crain was held in high regard by the citizens of Greenville. His favor also increased among the wider circle of Southern Baptists, and they soon elected him to the office of first vice-president of the Southern Baptist Convention.

All along, Dean Crain never forgot his humble Dark Corner roots. He visited family and friends up there often. In his sermons, he loved to reference his mountain youth and some of the experiences he had and the people he knew. In *A Mountain Boy's Life Story*, he wrote about the people of the Dark Corner and the significant challenges they faced:

> *The people of this section have been abused by newspaper and public speakers, and yet later developments have shown that a kindly interest and helpful hand was the thing they needed rather than abuse. They are a neglected people. They have the fine physique, good brains and are willing to learn if only given the chance. One of their chief traits of character is loyalty to each other. They stand by their convictions at any cost.*[15]

Dean Crain was always and forever an advocate for the folks of the Dark Corner and, as a result, had many friends there.

Crain served the congregation of Pendleton Street for twenty-one years before his retirement in 1952. On September 30, 1952, he was invited by South Carolina governor James F. Byrnes to travel to the statehouse in Columbia and deliver an invocation during a visit of President Dwight D. Eisenhower. A Washington newspaper reported of that day, "Enthusiastic as he was Governor Byrnes didn't match the fervor of Rev. Dean Crain, who prayed."[16]

On January 10, 1955, Dr. J. Dean Crain died peacefully in his sleep at his Greenville home. Immediately, accolades poured in from across the country. He was eulogized in the U.S. House of Representatives. Baptist papers from across the country sang his praises. But perhaps the greatest tribute to the boy from the Dark Corner came in the form of a letter that was sent to Mrs. Crain from the White House in Washington, D.C. President Eisenhower recalled his meeting with Dr. Crain on the steps of the capitol in Columbia. He wrote, "As I listened to his prayer on the steps of the capitol in Columbia, I was so impressed with his earnestness and his simplicity that I inquired about him and learned of the high esteem in which he was held throughout the state."[17]

And so, this mountain boy's life story had an amazing conclusion. From moonshine maker to esteemed Baptist preacher and statesman. J. Dean Crain's example, no doubt, inspired many young people from the Dark Corner to strive for more and better. And that influence is still being felt to this day.

5

BIG ALEC

There have been many legendary characters to come from the Dark Corner, both famous and infamous. One character who would qualify as both was the man simply known as Big Alec Campbell. Alexander was his given name, but it was shortened to Alec, and then the Big Alec came along to distinguish him from another Campbell known as Little Alec.

Big Alec was a true son of the Dark Corner. His forebears came to this country from Scotland via Ireland sometime between the years 1750 and 1755, settling first in Maryland. Thomas Campbell Sr. (1715–1788) was the first of this Campbell clan to touch American soil. Thomas's grandson John Campbell Sr. (1760–1830) was the first of the Campbells to come south, first settling in Bath County, Virginia, before eventually traveling down the Great Wagon Road to York County, South Carolina. John Sr.'s grandson John Landrum Campbell was the first of the Dark Corner Campbells, settling on Tugaloo Road and, with his wife, Nancy, rearing twelve children who would carry on the Campbell name and establish the Campbell family in the legend and lore of the Dark Corner. John Landrum's son Elford was the father of Big Alec Campbell.

Big Alec was born on September 2, 1883. These were hard times, to say the least, just a little less than twenty years after the Civil War. The era was marked by extreme poverty in this part of the country. Pellagra, a deadly yet highly preventable disease caused mainly by malnutrition, plagued many. In fact, Big Alec lost a sister to pellagra. Residents of the Dark Corner in those days not only faced disease but also fought the twin enemies of ignorance and vice. Though limited schooling of sorts was available, not everyone took advantage of those opportunities. Then there was the general chaos and violence often caused by the widespread abuse of alcohol. Liquor was so readily available because it was made illegally in the Dark Corner on such a large scale. This, in turn, brought about mayhem and murder.

This was the world Big Alec Campbell was born into. Although Big Alec's grandfather, for a time, ran a gristmill, the family's survival mainly depended on subsistence farming, attempting to grow corn and cotton on rocky, mineral-starved soil. It was never easy.

Big Alec married Tallie Center in 1910. They settled and built a home on several acres he had earlier purchased from his uncle Lafayette Campbell on State Highway 414, not far from Ebenezer-Welcome Baptist Church. There they raised a large family. Big Alec supported his growing family by farming, but it was no secret that a large portion of his income was derived from making illegal whiskey and operating several stills scattered here and there across the countryside.

Moonshine making was a lucrative business back in the day. As Dr. James Howard points out in *Dark Corner Heritage*,

> *If a man had a little corn for sale, he could not get more than 50 or 60 cents a bushel for it. Thus, there was a strong incentive and temptation to have the corn ground into meal and distilled into moonshine whiskey. A bushel of corn made about two-and one-half gallons of whiskey, selling for $1.00 per gallon, therefore, providing $2.50 per bushel instead of 50 or 60 cents.*[18]

Such financial facts of life inspired many a mountain man with a large and growing family to sell his corn by the gallon rather than by the bushel. This must have been the case with Big Alec Campbell. Big Alec seemed to be a target of the revenue officers. They had his number. But Big Alec's biggest problem was his own addiction to strong drink. He was his own worst enemy. Big Alec's son Troy once lamented that when his father drank, he seemed to lose all ability to reason and was, as a result, subject to fits of rage and violence. A couple of tragic episodes in his life are good examples of this.

It was 1919. The moonshine business had been especially lucrative that year. On Big Alec's side porch, just outside the kitchen, there stood a large steamer trunk where he kept the proceeds of his whiskey sales. It seemed to be no secret in the community that the trunk was brimming with cash, and so it was no surprise when it piqued the interest of one of Big Alec's hired hands. One, James Garvin, began taking a special interest in the money-laden trunk, and Big Alec's wife, Tallie, started noticing it. One afternoon, while Big Alec was away, Garvin stepped up onto the porch to help himself when he was encountered by Tallie. She wasted no time finding her husband, and Big Alec had been drinking. He retrieved his shotgun and went after Garvin. The stories differ at this point. Some say Campbell shot him point-blank without asking any questions, while Big Alec declared Garvin pulled a revolver and he shot him in self-defense. Big Alec and some of his friends

Home of Big Alec Campbell on Highway 414 in Landrum.

wasted no time in finding a homemade casket and quickly interring Garvin in an unmarked grave at Ebenezer-Welcome cemetery. An inquest was made into the shooting, and Big Alec's story of self-defense was believed and officially accepted. But many that day think Big Alec Campbell got away with murder.

But then in 1932, Campbell was implicated in still another murder. This time it was the murder of his wife, Tallie. The story goes like this, as told to me by Big Alec's grandson Jimmy Campbell, who heard it from his father, Troy, Big Alec's oldest son. Campbell and one of his friends, "Little Man" Painter, were both inebriated that day, and they were inside the Campbell home. It's unclear whether it was intentional or simply a terrible, unfortunate accident, but Big Alec was brandishing a loaded pistol. The gun discharged, and the round went through a wall, striking Tallie, who was in another room of the house. She was badly wounded. Two of her children carried her to an automobile and transported her to the home of Dr. Thomas Morrow, a genial country physician who lived just a few miles from the Campbell home. After a quick examination, Dr. Morrow knew that Tallie's wounds were most likely mortal, so he contacted the Petty Funeral Home, which, at that time, was nearby in Gowensville. Petty, as most funeral homes in that day did, operated an ambulance service, so help came immediately and transported Tallie to Mary Black Hospital in Spartanburg. There she lived for ten days and then died.

Big Alec would not escape arrest and conviction this time. He was convicted of the murder of his wife on September 1, 1932, and was sentenced to life imprisonment. Seven children were then left to fend for themselves, the older ones trying, as best they could, to care for the younger ones.

Mysteriously and unexpectedly, Big Alec's murder sentence was soon commuted to just four years, and then, in January 1935, he was paroled. The story goes that his oldest son, Troy, was directed to reach deep into the side porch steamer trunk and retrieve $2,000 in cash, an enormous sum in 1934. Then he was carefully instructed to carry the cash to Columbia, where he was to make contact with a high-ranking public official, who would then make sure the cash got to just the right person, who, in turn, orchestrated Big Alec's hasty parole. And once again, it appeared Big Alec seemed to get away with murder.

One would think that after all these brushes with the law that Big Alec Campbell would have learned his lesson and would retire to a life of peace, law and order. Not so. Big Alec returned to his liquor making and liquor drinking ways. Once again, he was arrested and brought up on federal charges of illegal distilling. He went to trial in Greenville with some others who had been apprehended for the same offense. On the day of his trial, he took his eight-year-old son Jake with him to the Greenville Court House for the proceedings. The *Greenville Piedmont* of that fateful afternoon gave an account of what took place:

> *Death brought a dramatic close in the trial of Alex Campbell, 54-year-old Gowensville farmer in the U.S. District Court here at 1:05 o'clock this afternoon as the black mustached defendant collapsed in the witness chair and died a few minutes later. The strange climax to a case in which Campbell was being tried on a federal charge of distilling was preceded by unusual remarks of the witness in the witness chair, in which his attorney, Hoke B. Black, said he must have felt a premonition of death. The attorney also said he had a strange feeling, and just before the defendant collapsed the attorney had stepped to Judge C.C. Wyche's bench and apologized for the defendant's answers to Assistant District Attorney E.P. Riley. Mr. Riley asked Campbell if he knew another defendant and Campbell replied, "I'd know him in hell." Mr. Riley, thinking he had not heard clearly asked him again and was given the same answer. Campbell's attorney, Mr. Black, also asked him the question and it seemed to confuse the defendant for a moment. When asked a third time, Campbell muttered, "My God." Judge Wyche interposed, "You can't use that language in this court." Then attorney Black stepped to the judge and apologized. Stepping to the front of the court, attorney Black asked him to come down from the chair, but Judge Wyche held him for a moment to ask if the government was finished. Attorney Riley agreed and Campbell was told to come down. As he started Campbell uttered one loud groan which startled the courtroom, then stiffened backward in the chair. Judge Wyche doffed his robe and called for the marshall and his deputies to attend him and dispatched another to bring a doctor. Dr. R.C. Bruce, who arrived a few minutes later examined Campbell, looked up and said, "There's nothing that can be done for this man." A boy in overalls, a son of Campbell, was brought in about 15 minutes later to take his father's effects, and red-eyed and sobbing the boy searched his dead father's pockets. The body was removed shortly afterward to a local mortuary. It was believed to be the first time in history that a defendant died in a courtroom in Greenville County.*[19]

Thus ended the life of the notorious Big Alec Campbell. Over the years, I have had the distinct privilege of knowing every one of Big Alec's children, with the exception of Jake (the son who was in the courtroom the day his father died and was killed several years later in a tragic automobile/train collision) and another son who died in childhood. And I was especially honored to participate in the funeral services of four of these children. And I can say that these were some of the finest, most upstanding people I have ever known. They were all actively involved in their churches, and each raised a fine family—an ironic twist to the tragic story of Big Alec Campbell.

6

THE MURDER OF A REVENUER

Dr. James A. Howard was an iconic figure in Dark Corner history. Born near the Highland community in 1894, he later became a well-known and highly respected Baptist minister who left the Dark Corner early on but returned later in life after retirement to live out his years with his beloved wife, Ruth, at their lovely Glassy Mountain Road home, which they affectionately named Pinebrook.

I first met Dr. Howard in 1982 when he was eighty-eight and I was twenty-eight. He was the long-retired pastor, and I was the brand-new young preacher at Ebenezer-Welcome Baptist Church, just right up the road from Pinebrook. We became good friends. Occasionally, he would hitch a ride with me to associational ministers' conferences, and I cherished our times together. I would visit him and Mrs. Howard and listen with rapt attention to his stories about his early days up in the Dark Corner. Just two years prior to our first meeting, at the tender age of eighty-six, he wrote the first comprehensive, albeit brief, history of the Dark Corner, which he titled *Dark Corner Heritage*. To assist him with the editing and artwork of this book, he called on a young friend of his named Dean Stuart Campbell, who would become his protégé and become known as the Squire of Dark Corner. Dean would also become a good friend of mine, and, shortly before his death, he did me the honor of writing the foreword to my book *North of Jordan*. *Dark Corner Heritage* was a book chockfull of history, stories and fascinating anecdotes that soon would have faded into oblivion had the elder Howard not chronicled them for posterity. *Dark Corner Heritage* remains a favorite of folks and has recently been reprinted, to the joy of so many.

Without a doubt, the most compelling of all Dark Corner stories was the story of Dr. Jim Howard himself. And, by the way, it was not even included in his book. It was the story of his courageous father and the ultimate price he paid for the sake of law and order. And it's a story well worth repeating.

Dr. Howard's father was James Holland Howard. A descendant of the far-famed Captain Thomas Howard, Holland Howard was born on September 18, 1872, in the heart of the Dark Corner. He and his wife, Elizabeth, reared a large family on a farm located between Glassy Mountain Baptist Church and the Highland community. The family were members of Highland Baptist Church.

Like so many Dark Corner families in those days, the Howards made and sold illegal whiskey. As did most hill country moonshiners at the time, the Howards felt that distilling was their own personal business as well as their God-given right. I remember Dr. Howard telling me how oftentimes they would be down on the branch making moonshine while Highland Baptist Church, where they were members, was having a summer revival meeting. He chuckled, "The church windows would be open, and the folks would be singing hymns with all their hearts, and we'd be down there working that mash and singing right along with 'em!"

At some point, a dramatic change took place in Howard's attitude toward moonshining. What spawned the change is anybody's guess. It could have been son Jim's Christian conversion and subsequent call to the ministry; nevertheless, the making of moonshine lost its attraction to Holland Howard. James Holland Howard abandoned the whiskey still to wear the badge of a state constable, whose job was to destroy illegal distilleries. For a former moonshiner to become a lawman was almost unthinkable in those days and was viewed by many moonshiners as an unpardonable sin. Oftentimes, those who made this transition, in effect, signed their own death warrant. Holland Howard placed himself in a perilous position when he did this.

We don't know that much about "Hol" Howard's "still busting" exploits prior to that fateful day of January 31, 1924, but as a lawman he must have been involved in a great many of them. January 31, 1924, must have dawned like any other midwinter day in the Dark Corner. Constable Howard prepared for another day of dangerous duty. His .45-caliber revolver was loaded and close to his side. In all probability, he was also carrying a Winchester carbine, a favorite of lawmen in that era. Howard and his son Clarence, who had been deputized for duty that day, joined federal narcotics agents E.N. Austin and Reuben Gosnell for a routine raid at the foot of Hogback Mountain alongside the South Pacolet River. On the way to their destination, the team encountered two Plumley brothers whom they suspected had been busy at the still that morning. The pair were arrested and placed in the custody of Austin and young Howard, who locked the suspects in a nearby corncrib.

Holland Howard and Agent Gosnell carefully proceeded to the site of the still and separated as they edged closer so Gosnell could cut off any attempted escape of those who might already be busy at the still that morning. Unbeknownst to the lawmen Alex Pittman and his son Holland were hiding in a cave close by. This is when they opened fire on Holland Howard. Howard was struck five times, both front and back. His wounds were mortal. Gosnell pursued the shooters. Alex Pittman escaped, and Reuben Gosnell engaged Holland Pittman in a fierce gun battle that ended with Pittman's surrender. Three suspects, the two Plumley brothers and Holland Pittman, were all escorted to the Greenville County jail. Alex Pittman later surrendered to the authorities.

Dr. Howard shared with me how he first heard of his father's death. He was a student at Furman at the time, where he was studying for the ministry. He was also a member of the Furman football team. Someone notified him on campus that day of his father's tragic end. Without delay, he immediately made his way back home to Highland, and he said when he arrived, they were just bringing his father's bullet-ridden body from the foot of Hogback in the back of a two-horse wagon. He recalled, "I got there and there was a crowd around the wagon peering down on my father's lifeless body. And all of a sudden somebody in the crowd blurted out, 'That shore was a purty shot!'" I cannot imagine how I would have responded to such a heartless remark, but evidently the young preacher took it in stride and walked away. His father would be buried in the Highland Baptist Church cemetery, where, many years later, Dr. Howard himself would be interred.

Just a couple of weeks later, the grieving son wrote a letter to the editor of the *Greenville News* decrying the terrible blight of the moonshine industry on the people of the Dark Corner. The letter was dated February 17, 1924:

> *Dear Editor:*
> *Please let me say a word through your paper about the breeding place of crime in Greenville County. Since the murder of my father on January 31, while assisting Prohibition agents Gosnell and Austin to raid a moonshine still in the "Dark Corner", I have tried to locate the breeding places of crime.*

> *I believe that without a doubt that the worst breeding place, in these parts, is at the blockader's still. There the seed of murder is sown in the hearts of the moonshiners because he hates the people who are against his business. He hates the officer who tries to enforce the law. At the moonshiner's still candidates for the jailhouse, penitentiary and electric chair are bred, regard for law and order is forgotten and sanctity for womanhood is set aside. The moonshiner is not altogether to blame for if it were not for his faithful customers he would have to go out of business. The man that buys a keg of whiskey and transports it to town, transports more than whiskey alone. He transports that which causes sorrow, heartaches, tears, empty pocketbooks, poverty-stricken homes, ignorance, preventable diseases, and immorality. The citizen, judge, lawyer, or officer that upholds, sympathizes, drinks, or shields in any shape or form is cultivating and fertilizing the breeding places of crime. Such a man is an enemy to humanity, the yet unborn, the home, the churches, and the State. If the citizenship would demand absolute duty from the judge's bench, the juror's box, the lawyer's office and the officer's quarters, there would be less crime and sin. But so long as there is folding of hands some of the above places will be breeding places of crime.*
> *Jim Howard*[20]

Howard's emotional appeal concludes with his call for strict enforcement of laws on the books and for judges, jurors and lawyers to quit assisting moonshiners by tolerating their activity and buying their product.

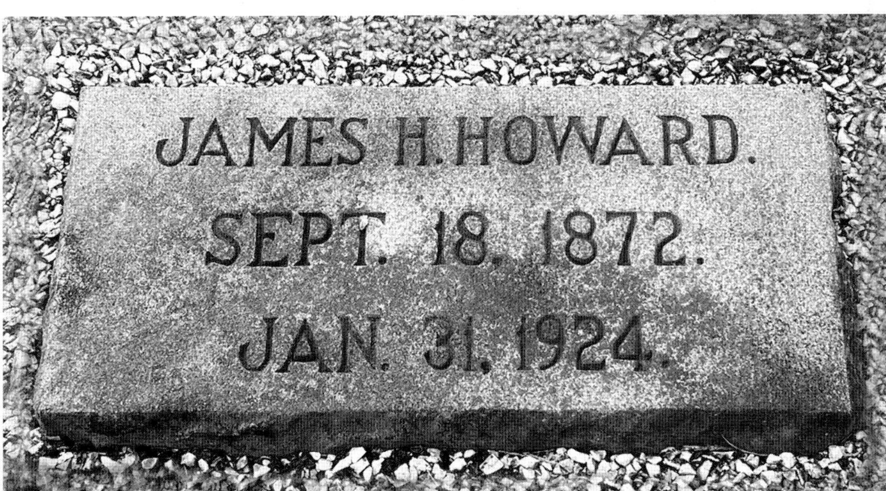

Tombstone of Holland Howard in the Highland Baptist Church cemetery.

Both Holland and Alexander Pittman were found guilty of the death of Constable Howard. Solicitor David W. Smoak sought the death penalty. There seemed to be overwhelming public support for the execution of the Pittmans. A mournful, tear-jerking murder ballad called "The Ballad of Holland Howard" started making the rounds, further inflaming public opinion against the Pittmans. Both men were found guilty of murder by a jury of their peers on May 17, 1924. Their case was appealed all the way to the South Carolina Supreme Court, and the court upheld the decision on September 26, 1926. Governor Thomas G. McLeod signed the death warrant, which was to be carried out on October 29, 1926. By a strange turn of events, including letters to the governor pleading for clemency for the Pittmans from the prosecutors of the case, the governor granted a stay of execution just two days before the pair were to be put to death in the electric chair. A report in the *Greenville News* from Wednesday, October 27, 1926, gives the governor's reasons for granting clemency to the convicted murderers:

> *Whenever the issue of life and death is involved in a case it is necessarily more serious and I know of no limitations to the seriousness of the consideration to be given in such cases. The appeal of the Pittman's, father, and son has been presented to me upon the record in the case, a most numerously signed petition, and a large number of letters of citizens, whose interests have been aroused. As I conceive the duties of the Chief Magistrate, it is expressed in the constitution. He shall take care that the laws be executed in mercy. After the very careful and painstaking consideration I have given to the Pittman's appeal it is sufficient to say that under all circumstances, as I know them, it is my conviction that the extreme penalty of the law should not be meted out in this case. I can do nothing but follow this conviction. I have therefore commuted the sentence to imprisonment in the State penitentiary for life.*

In an even stranger twist of events, both Pittmans were paroled on October 5, 1933, for "good behavior." And on January 5, 1935, Governor Ibra C. Blackwood pardoned Holland and Alex Pittman. Blackwood will be remembered as being the same governor who freed Big Alec Campbell.

Agent Reuben Gosnell, who was present the day Holland Howard was killed, went on to become a U.S. marshal, appointed by President Franklin D. Roosevelt on the recommendation of then U.S. senator from South Carolina James F. Byrnes. A humorous story about Marshal Gosnell was told to me by the eminent historian of Upper Greenville County, the late

Mann Batson. It was told to him by J. Dean Crain Jr., otherwise known as Jim or Jimmy by his friends and acquaintances. At the time of this story, Jimmy Crain was working on the staff of Marshal Reuben Gosnell, mostly serving as a driver. Crain told of a day when he and Gosnell were transporting a prisoner to the federal penitentiary in Atlanta. It was close to Thanksgiving, and the pair were returning from the prison and were driving down a backcountry Georgia road when they happened to pass upon a turkey farm located on the rural Georgia highway. Gosnell, according to Crain, spoke with a high, nasal twang, and he told his young driver, "Jimmy, pull over here. I'm going to buy Senator Byrnes a Thanksgiving turkey." Crain complied and guided the government vehicle onto the dusty, rocky driveway. Gosnell got out of the car and struck up a conversation with the poultry farmer and told him he wanted to purchase the largest, fattest gobbler he had. The farmer returned with a large, live turkey that Gosnell stuffed into the trunk of his car, and the pair returned to Greenville with a gobbling gobbler in the trunk. They traveled directly to the train depot, where the ill-fated turkey was crated and shipped by rail to Senator Byrnes in Washington. Crain recalled a few days later Marshal Gosnell receiving a telegram from the senator thanking him for his feathered gift. But, the senator added, "If you ever send another turkey up this way, please send a smaller one. We couldn't find a roasting pan big enough to cook him!" Gosnell looked at his young protégé and shook his head, saying, "Jimmy, can you imagine that in all of Washington, D.C., they couldn't find a pot big enough to cook that turkey in?"

Reuben Gosnell died peacefully at the age of seventy-three on June 12, 1948, and was buried alongside his first wife in Graceland Cemetery in Greenville.[21]

I wanted to share a tender conclusion to this tragic story that I personally witnessed many years ago. It was sometime in the early 1980s when I was pastor of Ebenezer-Welcome Baptist Church in Landrum. There was a funeral that day, and graveside services in the church cemetery were concluding. I glanced over and saw a scene I have never forgotten. Dr. Jim Howard, the son of Constable Holland Howard, was talking cordially with a daughter of Holland Howard's accused killer, Alex Pittman. Her father allegedly killed his father, but instead of harboring feelings of animosity toward one another, there they stood speaking like the old friends they were. And that day in that country graveyard, I learned a great and vivid lesson on grace and forgiveness.

7
THUNDER IN THE MOUNTAINS

It was touted to be the war to end all wars. Of course, it didn't accomplish its goal, but it was the first global conflict that the United States was involved in. Through a series of key events, culminating with the assassination of Austrian archduke Franz Ferdinand on June 28, 1914, Europe became embroiled in fierce combat of epic proportions in August 1914. America, geographically detached from the fighting, was able to remain out of the war for three years. But because of accelerated submarine attacks on U.S. merchant vessels, the sinking of the *Lusitania* in 1915 and the German invasion of Belgium, America could no longer remain neutral. So, on April 4, 1917, the U.S. Senate drew up resolutions of war against Germany, and two days later the House followed suit. The United States had officially entered World War I.

With this declaration of war, the country kicked into overdrive in establishing wartime industry and war support efforts. And obviously, millions of new soldiers had to be trained for combat. Antiquated existing military bases were woefully inadequate for handling the tremendous flow of manpower and material needed for the mass mobilization. Cities and towns across the country were competing for the opportunity to play host to one of these new military facilities. Both Greenville and Spartanburg were also in the hunt. Greenville was awarded Camp Sevier, and Spartanburg became home to Camp Wadsworth.

Spartanburg's city fathers and most prominent politicians joined forces in wooing the Department of War. But it may very well have been the local

Episcopal rector who tipped the scale in Spartanburg's favor. Reverend W.H.K. Pendleton was the rector of Spartanburg's historic Episcopal Church of the Advent. Years before coming to Spartanburg, Pendleton taught in an Episcopal school in Virginia, and it just so happened that one of his star students was Newton D. Baker, who would eventually become President Woodrow Wilson's secretary of war.

On June 21, 1917, the city of Spartanburg learned that it would become home to the U.S. Army's Camp Wadsworth, named for Union general James S. Wadsworth, who was mortally wounded during the Battle of the Wilderness on May 8, 1864. Soon thereafter, a two-thousand-acre tract of land on the west side of Spartanburg was leased by the federal government to serve as home to the military base. Most of the land consisted of new-growth forests and cotton fields with long exhausted soil. After the papers were signed on June 4, 1917, construction began in earnest.

Of course, the sleepy textile town of Spartanburg was barely ready for the onslaught of soldiers and civilian workers who would converge on the town in droves. In 1917, Spartanburg had a population of just 20,000. Before it was all said and done, an estimated 100,000 people would come through Camp Wadsworth. And while Wadsworth proved to be a definite boon to the Spartanburg economy, it did, in fact, place a huge strain on local infrastructure and services.

There were three army divisions that called Camp Wadsworth home: the 6th, the 96th and the 27th. The U.S. Army's 27th Division was composed mainly of troops from the New York National Guard. It was comprised the 102nd Mortar Battery and the 104th, 105th and 106th Field Artillery Regiments. The 27th trained and remained at Camp Wadsworth until dispatched to France for combat in May 1918.

One of the most obvious requirements for an artillery unit is an artillery range. Some of the firepower the 27th employed had a range up to seven miles, thus requiring a sparsely populated area and plenty of space to lob the powerful shells. This, of course, would be impossible in or anywhere around the camp itself. So, after a careful search, the War Department settled on a large tract of land in northern Greenville County in the heart of the Dark Corner. Glassy and Hogback Mountains and the ridges below would serve as suitable targets for the heavy field artillery, but rifle ranges would also be designed and constructed for the smaller caliber weapons.

Naturally, people who lived near the range would have to be relocated for safety purposes, and that would be a gargantuan task to make lease agreements with people who were already suspicious of the outsiders who

Hogback Mountain.

were invading their territory. Especially northerners, just fifty years after the conclusion of the Civil War! And yet it was a time in the nation when most people, both North and South, were sympathetic to the war effort. Many historians view World War I as one of the most important unifying factors that helped bring the nation closer together after being torn apart by the Civil War. U.S. Army captain Cornelius W. Wickersham was given the assignment of securing leases from the mountain people, no easy task.[22] Finally, by September 1917, most people who were required to move had moved. A seven-by-three-mile swath of land was needed for the range. It was obtained, and the 22nd Engineers then moved in and began designing rifle and artillery ranges and digging a series of trenches similar to the ones being used in France.

The infantry of the 27th Division was called on to do the lion's share of the work on the Glassy/Hogback artillery and rifle range. To give some modern perspective as to where most of the activity was taking place, one would need to travel west on SC Highway 11 from Gowensville. Approximately two miles from the Gowensville crossing, at the intersection of Highway 11 and Dill Road, is where the bulk of the artillery battery was located. Cannons and long-range field guns were fired across Chestnut Ridge toward the mountains, with most of the rounds falling near the South Pacolet River. Farther west on Highway 11 is where the rifle ranges were situated. Troops were bivouacked on the east side of Dill Road. Remembering that at this time Highway 11 was merely a narrow, muddy or dusty country road, barely passable at times, gives one a much greater appreciation for how the men of the 27th Division were able to make the journey all the way from Camp Wadsworth in Spartanburg to the foot of Glassy Mountain. Supplies and heavy equipment were often transported by rail from Spartanburg to Landrum or Campobello. Then, sometimes with great difficulty, cargo would be moved to the range by mule-driven wagons or trucks. Some men and supplies were hauled by truck from Camp Wadsworth. But for the most part, the foot soldiers would march the twenty-six-mile distance from Camp Wadsworth to the artillery range at the foot of the Blue Ridge mountains. It has been suggested that at the beginning of the soldiers' training it took them a good three days to make the rigorous journey on foot, stopping along the way to camp. But after training and physical conditioning, they often made the march in a single day. Most likely the route they followed from the west side of Spartanburg began on Blackstock Road, taking them to New Cut Road. New Cut took them all the way to Highway 11 near Gowensville, and from there it was a short two-mile march to the range.

There are a number of interesting stories about the interactions the New Yorkers would have with the local civilians along the way. One of my personal favorites is a romantic tale involving a young GI from upstate New York. His

Site of an old World War I gunnery trench just off of Highway 11.

name was Spencer Christman, and on one of those grueling marches from Camp Wadsworth to the range at Glassy, as the troops traveled down New Cut Road, they stopped either to camp or just for a break to rest near a small

Intersection of Holly Springs Road and New Cut Road in Spartanburg County. This is the location of the old country store operated by Mae Blackwell's father when she first met Private Christman.

country store located at the intersection of New Cut Road and Holly Springs Road. While there, Spencer met a pretty blonde southern belle named Mae Blackwell. Her father owned and operated the little crossroads general store. During this brief encounter Cupid struck, igniting romantic feelings in the hearts of the young soldier and the pretty local lass. Some would call it love at first sight, and indeed, it was. Contact information was exchanged, and letters were written. During Spencer's time of service in France, there were letters almost every day from New Cut Road. When Spencer returned home, the courtship resumed in earnest, and in 1921 Spencer Christman and Mae Blackwell were married, living happily ever after! There must have been many stories like this of romances between lonely, homesick GIs and the local girls who met them along the way. There are also stories of busy housewives in the area of the artillery range who made extra money baking pies, cakes and cookies to sell to the soldiers camped close to their homes.

So, from September 1917 until April 1918, when the artillery range ceased operation, there was a whole lot of man-made thunder rocking the ridges, valleys and the mountains of the Dark Corner. The 27th Division departed Camp Wadsworth in May 1918, crossing over to France to participate in the fighting. Some from that division never returned home. They were buried honorably in the land where they had fallen for the cause of liberty.

Soon, the displaced residents of Glassy and Hogback returned to their homes in the hills that had been pockmarked by heavy artillery rounds. Some of those people never returned to the mountain. And the army began removing the last vestiges of military occupation. Trenches were filled or left untouched. Gun emplacements were removed. For years after this, residents continued to find spent and empty artillery shells, and occasionally they found a live round. I remember when I was serving as a pastor in the Dark Corner several years ago, I would often visit older church members who still had vivid memories of the artillery range in their backyard and might even have an old artillery shell on display on a table or shelf. Sometimes these empty shells were turned up by a plow or simply found in an open ditch. They were visible reminders of a time when doughboys from New York rambled through the hills and hollers of the Dark Corner. And one can only imagine what it must have been like in those days of 1917 or early 1918 as the sun set brilliantly over the western hills and a lone bugler played the haunting strains of taps over the tents pitched row by row in this quiet, isolated niche of the Dark Corner.

8

A JAIL BREAK TO REMEMBER

One of the most notorious and ruthless killings ever to take place in the Dark Corner was the murder of Benjamin Ross in February 1888. Ben Ross was a young husband and father of two who made a good living distilling corn whiskey. What set Ross apart from most of the other Dark Corner distillers was the fact that he made his liquor legally and with the government's approval.

A couple of different factors led to Ross's tragic and untimely death. The first was the price of the whiskey he was selling. At that time, illegal moonshine was selling for \$1.00 a gallon. Ross's legally made whiskey was selling for just \$0.50 more at \$1.50 a gallon. The reason this raised the ire of the illegal moonshiners was that customers, for the most part, would rather buy legal moonshine for a variety of reasons. First, they were willing to pay a premium price because there was less risk involved. You weren't likely to be trapped in a federal still raid while buying your gallon. Also, the quality of legal liquor was better because it was held to a higher standard by inspectors and tax collectors. So, Ross's legal and aboveboard business was not winning him friends among the other distillers. In addition to all this, some suspected him of reporting illegal moonshine activities to federal agents. This was speculation, but it all sealed Benjamin Ross's fate.

The Greenville newspaper of that day, the *Enterprise and Mountaineer*, published Mary Ross's sworn statement as to what took place at her home on that fateful February evening. This testimony appeared in the February 8 edition:

> *Just before six o'clock on yesterday evening, my husband, Benjamin Ross, after eating his supper, lay down before the fire. I heard the dogs bark. My little daughter went to the door but saw no one. She shut the door and came back to the fire, and then a gun fired outside the house, and the load struck him in the bowels. He then arose to his feet, put his hands on his breast and exclaimed, "Lord, have mercy. Harriet, I'm shot." He walked about six steps across the house and fell to his knees. He said again, "Lord, have mercy on me." He then breathed a few breaths in my arms and died. The gun was fired through the window from the piazza. No one was present in the house but myself and two children. I heard William Howard say he would shoot Ben Ross, my husband. This is Mr. Wade Howard's son William. These threats were made the first of last week to Thos. Rochester and James Moon.*[23]

So, it was no mystery about who killed Ben Ross. William Howard was immediately implicated in the murder. The only real question was, which William Howard? That's right. There were two William Howards, and both men had motive as well as opportunity to commit the horrific crime. One Howard was known by all as Big Bill Howard, and the other was, as you might have guessed, Little Bill Howard. Evidently, the two were first cousins. Big Bill was taller and stockier than his more diminutive kinsman. Both Bills were at the Ross home on the night of the murder, but their stories differed sharply. Not surprisingly, Little Bill implicated his cousin, testifying that Big Bill was, in fact, the trigger man. Then he claimed that Big Bill had threatened him on numerous occasions if he didn't agree to shoot Ben Ross with the double-barreled shotgun that was used in the murder. The whole story was so confusing and convoluted that both men were finally charged with the murder. At the trial held in July 1890, Big Bill was acquitted of the killing, but Little Bill was sentenced to death for the murder of Benjamin Ross. Little Bill was sentenced to hang for his crime in Greenville on September 26, 1890. Soon he was granted a stay of execution but remained in jail. What happened next was nothing short of amazing and became a great source of embarrassment for law enforcement, especially for Sheriff P.D. Gilreath, who had custody of the criminal at the time.

Little Bill's wife, Mary, petitioned Sheriff Gilreath for a weekend visit in jail with her husband. She also planned to bring their little daughter to spend some time with her jailed daddy. Gilreath, a sympathetic man, well known for his acts of kindness, granted her unorthodox request. Mary Howard and her daughter arrived at the Greenville jail on Saturday evening,

October 4. Little Bill greeted his wife and child, and the jailer left the trio alone in the small cell. Early on Monday morning, October 6, Little Bill called for the jailer to open the cell door so Mary and the baby could leave and return home. As were most mountain women of that day, Mary was attired in a long dress with an oversized bonnet, partly covering her face. She exited the cell. Later that morning, when the jailer came to bring Howard's breakfast, he was shocked to find Mary in the cell instead of Little Bill. She was wearing Little Bill's clothes! And Little Bill had made his escape wearing his wife's long dress and bonnet. He also had his young daughter in tow. The *Enterprise and Mountaineer* called it "one of the most audacious jail deliveries that has ever taken place in the county." It was, indeed, audacious, bold and incredibly imaginative.

Grave of Big Bill Howard at Glassy Mountain Baptist Church Cemetery. *Courtesy of Ralph Howard.*

Little Bill beat a hasty retreat to the Dark Corner. He left his little daughter and his disguise with a friend in Greenville and then headed for the hills. Mary was released a little later, and the wily Little Bill continued to evade law officers for about six months. Finally, word reached Sheriff Gilreath that Howard had been seen around his mother-in-law's home on several occasions. The sheriff and his deputies traveled to the Dark Corner and made a daring arrest of Little Bill, who was reported to be armed to the teeth. He put up little resistance, though, and was handily apprehended, and then remanded, once again, to the Greenville Jail, where he was watched with the greatest of vigilance.

In a surprising postscript to this remarkable story, the South Carolina Supreme Court granted Little Bill a new trial, and because of the death of a key witness, along with other mitigating circumstances, Little Bill Howard was acquitted. Both Little Bill and Big Bill were free men. A little over two months later, though, Big Bill Howard would meet his demise at the hand of another first cousin named George Center. Center was meaning to avenge the murder of Ben Ross, who was also Center's stepfather. He met Big Bill on a narrow Dark Corner lane. Words were exchanged, and thinking Big Bill was reaching into his pocket to retrieve a knife or pistol, Center shot Big Bill point-blank with a .22-caliber rifle. Howard survived for a day before succumbing to his wounds. Though indicted for the murder, Center was eventually acquitted because it was determined he acted in self-defense.[24]

Thus closed another bloody chapter in Dark Corner history. Dr. Jim Howard offered an interesting and humorous conclusion to this story years later. He was speaking one evening to a group, and his topic was Dark Corner history. His book *Dark Corner Heritage* had just been published, and he was much in demand as a speaker on the subject. When he completed his presentation, he stayed behind to greet those who had attended and answer any individual questions they might have. That night, Howard went into detail about the murder of Ben Ross. As people were leaving, he noticed an elderly woman remaining behind, obviously wanting to talk to him. He approached her, and she offered him her hand. As he shook it, she looked up at him, grinning, and said, "I was the baby Pa carried out of the Greenville jail!"

9
A TENDER FAREWELL

The name Barton is a familiar one in the Dark Corner and the upper part of Greenville County. Several generations of Bartons have called this beautiful section of the country home. The family's progenitor, John Barton, originated in England and settled in Virginia early in the colonial era.[25] One of his sons was David Barton, a veteran of the American Revolution and the first of the Barton clan to head south and settle in the sparsely populated northwest corner of South Carolina. Family tradition proudly recounts the heroic deeds of David Barton during the Revolutionary War, including a few occasions when he narrowly eluded capture by the British.[26] When he moved into the Greenville District, he began buying land and soon became a man of some means. David had seven sons, and one of those sons was Wilson Barton, the subject of this chapter.

Wilson, much like his father before him, was ambitious and began purchasing several large tracts of land. It also helped that he married well. In 1819, he wed Mildah McKinney, the daughter of Alexander McKinney, one of the more prominent men in the area at that time. Not long after they married, Wilson was able to purchase two hundred acres of land near the Head of Tyger Church, now Tyger Baptist Church. He settled into the life of a country squire, and he and Mildah raised a family of seven sons and three daughters. The Bartons became members of Head of Tyger Church.

At the time of Wilson Barton's marriage to Mildah, the State Road was proposed, running from the busy markets of Charleston and Columbia, up through Greenville and on to the mountains of North Carolina. Wilson's interest in the road came not only from the fact that such a road would bring commerce and prosperity to the area, but more especially because the proposed route ran close to his father-in-law's property, so he saw this as an opportunity for everyone to profit.

There's evidence that one of the road's principal designers and supervisors, Joel Roberts Poinsett, became a close friend of Barton's. In fact, Barton named one of his sons Joel Poinsett Barton. He also made his childhood home available to Poinsett while the work on the road was going on.[27] Poinsett, who was an advisor to President Andrew Jackson, took a strong stand for the federal union during the Nullification Crisis of 1832, which may partly explain why Barton himself took such a strong posture against nullification.

The Nullification Crisis of 1832 resulted from a federal tariff imposed on goods shipped into the united States from abroad. This tariff would have put an undue tax burden on the South since it imported most of its manufactured goods. So, already some thirty years before the outbreak of the Civil War, there was growing animosity between North and South. Cotton growers who wielded so much power and influence in South Carolina knew they would be feeling th eeffects of this tariff. An economic downturn in the country at about this same time made the situation even worse. Some state leaders were even calling for secession and military action, if necessary.[28] Fortunately, for a time at least, cooler heads prevailed. But the consequences for Wilson Barton would be far-reaching.

Wilson Barton, like every other able-bodied man in South Carolina at that time, was a member in good standing of the South Carolina State Militia. The militia was a well-organized statewide military organization that was formed by mandate of the U.S. Congress in 1792 for the local defense and for the corporate defense of the country.[29] Before the Civil War, when the Black population exceeded the white population in the state, the militia was also viewed as an important deterrent against slave rebellions. The various militia units around the state were well armed, well organized and well trained. Each district had its own units, or beats, that met regularly to drill. Oftentimes these militia "musters" became social gatherings where political speeches were sometimes made, and officers were elected by popular vote.

In 1829, Wilson Barton was elected colonel of his regiment by his peers. This was a title he would proudly carry with him for the remainder of his life, even after he moved to Texas and was no longer associated with the state militia. Between the years 1832 and 1835, there was a strong sentiment in the state of South Carolina in support of nullification and even secession if deemed necessary. There were also those, particularly in the upstate, who supported the federal union. A definite divide was taking place.

Again, Wilson Barton was an unabashed Unionist, as were many in the Dark Corner. The reader will recall mention of Governor Perry's speech at Glassy Mountain Baptist Church, where he referred to the fact that the Dark Corner earned its famous name from supporters of nullification who claimed the people in that part of the country were "in the dark" because they opposed nullification. Barton's support of the Union would change his life significantly.

In 1835, a militia encampment was announced for Pickensville, which was, at that time, a hotbed of support for nullification. Some of the pro-Union militia leaders were concerned that the ulterior motive of this gathering was to put together a states rights army that would be used to defend the state against federal attack. President Jackson had already threatened military action against his home state should they ignore the tariff. As a result, some of those leaders who harbored pro-Union sentiments refused to attend the encampment. Colonel Wilson Barton was one of those who was reluctant to appear in Pickensville. It was then announced that those militia leaders who refused to come to Pickensville would be court-martialed. So, instead of going through the shame and spectacle of a public court-martial, Barton chose to resign his commission.[30] This decision, no doubt, caused him much grief and regret in the days ahead. And this event may very well have spawned Barton's departure from the state.

No one is exactly sure when Colonel Barton began contemplating a move, but it would not be surprising if the nullification controversy didn't have something to do with it, even though his move to Texas wouldn't come for another decade. Around the time of the Nullification Crisis (1832–33), a sharp economic downturn spurred a large migration of people westward. Many, about this time, moved to Alabama, some to Mississippi and Louisiana. Some of this migration was also a result of cotton planters abandoning the tired and worn-out soil of the state for the more fertile and loamy soils of the Mississippi delta. And after the defeat of Santa Anna, many South Carolinians began moving west to Texas. Reports were coming back to the state of plenty of available and fertile farmland at the right price. Undoubtedly, these optimistic reports reached Wilson Barton, and he was ready to make a change. He soon began selling his large tracts of land. But on September 25, 1848, tragedy struck the family when Barton's beloved wife died, leaving the grief-stricken husband with a one-year-old son. Mildah's death delayed the family's move to Texas, but it never left his mind.

Shelter covering the grave of Mildah Barton in the Tyger Baptist Church cemetery.

Finally, in the fall of 1854, a wagon train of ten or fifteen families formed in the Tigerville area to make the long, arduous journey west.[31] It must have been an impressive sight indeed as these pioneers embarked from the Dark Corner on their great adventure, which would end in Williamson County, Texas that December.

Colonel Wilson Barton prospered in Texas, but before he left, there was one last act of devotion and love he would perform for his late wife, Mildah. And if you wander through the cemetery of the Tyger Baptist Church today, you will still see his last tribute on display there. For there, prominently positioned in the middle of the churchyard ,is a monument to Mildah. It is a raised brick crypt with a weathered and worn marble slab atop it with Mildah's name, birth date and death date inscribed on it, now barely legible. But what catches your attention is the rustic enclosure around the grave. It is a shelter of sorts, made of sturdy black locust posts with a shingled roof over it. It was almost as if the husband, who knew he would most likely never return to this sacred spot, was performing one last act of love and devotion by sheltering his beloved wife's grave from the elements.

Over the years, members of the Barton family have returned to pay tribute to this beloved matriarch whom they left behind. The roof has been re-shingled on several occasions, but as of the 175th anniversary of its construction, it still stands as a tribute and testimony of a man's undying love for his wife he had to leave behind.

10

THE BOY FROM HORSE CREEK

Just across the mountains that serve as the northern border of the Dark Corner and on into North Carolina stands a peak called Skyuka. Named in honor of the Cherokee warrior who assisted Captain Thomas Howard in his defeat of the Indians at the Battle of Round Mountain in 1776, it also marks the birthplace of a true American legend. It was here in 1787 that "Old Bill" Williams, as he was popularly known, was born, just where Horse Creek runs into the Pacolet River.

Old Bill was a mountain man, renowned as an adventurer, trapper, hunter and Indian fighter. In his day, he was as well-known as his more famous contemporaries like Jim Bridger and Kit Carson.

Born in Polk County, North Carolina, on January 3, 1787, he was the fourth child of Joseph and Sarah Musick Williams. His father had served in the American Revolution before settling down at the foot of Skyuka. Bill, who was born William Sherley Williams, was raised like most boys in his day along the southern frontier. He learned early on to hunt in the rolling green hills of Polk County and fish in the crystal-clear waters of the Pacolet. It was during these early days that young Bill developed a lifelong love and adoration for the great outdoors. And he eagerly explored the mountains and foothills surrounding his beautiful and primitive home.

When he was eight years old, his family picked up and moved to St. Louis, Missouri. The year was 1795, and St. Louis, in those days, was truly the gateway to the great vastness of the unknown western frontier. No doubt, as a child, Bill watched with wonder as pioneers in wagons and on horseback disappeared across the Mississippi River into the great American wilderness beyond. It must have been here that the boy from Horse Creek was first bitten by the bug of wanderlust. Bill's parents made sure their son received a respectable education for his day and time. It was in St. Louis the boy learned to read and write, which was more than many of his mountain man contemporaries would accomplish.

At seventeen, Bill experienced a Christian conversion. Soon he took his Bible, mounted his horse and rode the circuit, living his life as an itinerant preacher. He preached in rural churches across Missouri, earning the nickname "Parson Williams," which, along with "Old Bill," would remain with him for the rest of his days.[32]

During the War of 1812, he joined the U.S. Army and put to good use his considerable skills as a tracker and guide. In these days, he became familiar with the ways of the Native American tribes on the plains. He lived and worked among the Osage, marrying an Osage woman and fathering two daughters.[33] It was also during this time that his attention turned from preaching the gospel to trapping and selling choice fur pelts. His pursuit of these pelts carried him further and further into western territories, often uncharted territories, which only added to his legend.

As his reputation grew, so did the demand for him to guide western adventurers and act as a go-between with the Indians. His towering stature and his fiery red hair made him stand out and only added to his mystique among the Indians. And the Native American tribes of the West came to honor and respect this white man who knew so much about them and their time-honored ways.

Old Bill's most famous, or infamous, adventure was the Fremont Expedition of 1848. American soldier and politician John Fremont had been given the assignment by the U.S. government to find a route through the wilderness for the railroad to connect St. Louis with San Francisco, which would have been a formidable task in 1848. When this party reached Pueblo, Colorado, Fremont engaged Bill Williams to guide them to California.

Winter was fast approaching, and Williams strongly urged Fremont not to proceed and certainly not to take the route he had in mind through a snow-filled pass. Fremont refused Old Bill's counsel, and the expedition went on ahead through the treacherous and icy pass. Soon they found themselves snowbound in the San Juan Mountains. Bill Williams and two others retreated from the pass at great peril to themselves to get help for the stranded travelers. In the meantime, ten members of Fremont's group perished from hunger and exposure. Eventually, Fremont himself and other

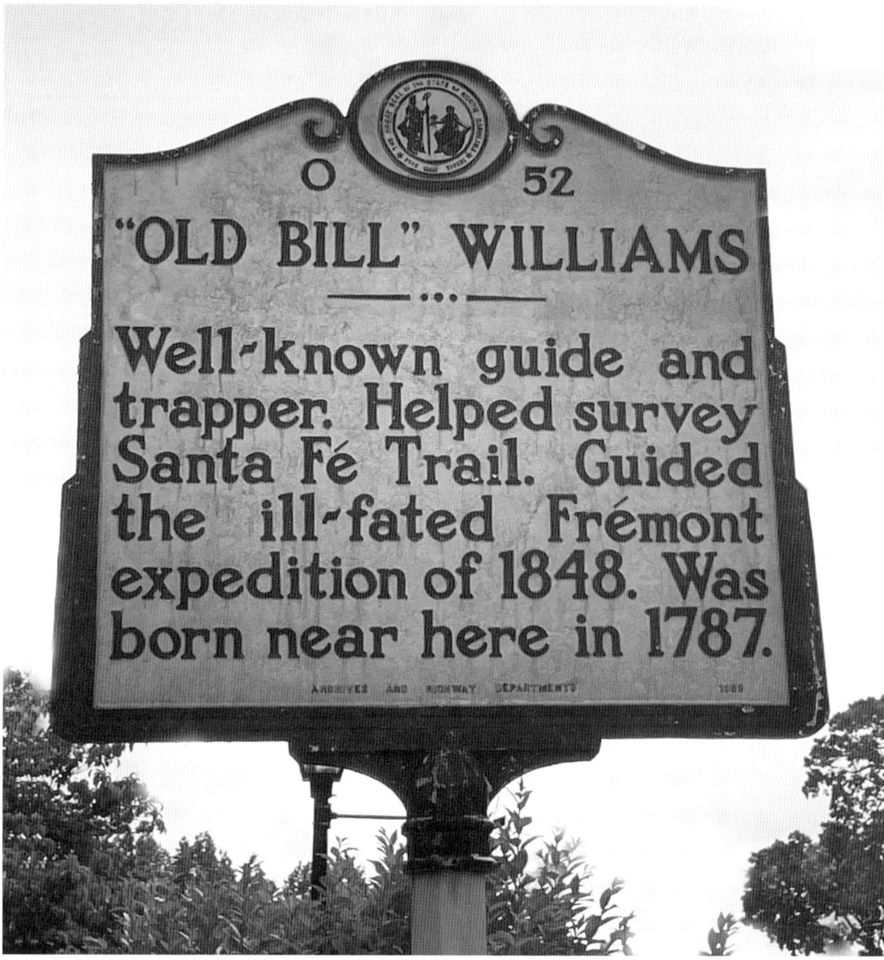

Historical marker in Columbus, North Carolina, telling the story of Old Bill Williams.

survivors of this horrendous ordeal ventured on and reached Taos, New Mexico, and then continued to California. After reaching California and receiving so much public criticism for leading this expedition through much danger and peril, Fremont then tried to place the greatest part of the blame for the disaster on Bill Williams. He even accused the mountain man of cannibalism, a charge that was later disproved, but not before it severely damaged the great guide's reputation and pride.[34]

Old Bill Williams met his own demise less than a year after the Fremont debacle. On March 14, 1849, Williams and a companion were hunting in

Colorado when they were ambushed by a party of Utes. Williams had always been on friendly terms with the Utes, and it was only after they went to scalp him that they recognized his thick mane of red hair. The Utes immediately realized they had made a terrible and tragic mistake by killing their old friend.[35] As a result, they buried Old Bill with all the pomp and ceremony of a great chief. For generations, Bill Williams was celebrated among the Utes as a great, celebrated hero.

Today, the boy from Horse Creek is memorialized by an eight-foot statue in his likeness in Bill Williams Monument Park in Williams, Arizona. There is also the Bill Williams River and Bill Williams Mountain in Arizona. The only reminder of the boy from Horse Creek in his home state of North Carolina is a historical marker that stands in the town square of Columbus, North Carolina, not many miles from the foot of Skyuka, where Horse Creek makes its way into the Pacolet, just across the green hills from the Dark Corner.

II

GRINDING CORN IN THE DARK CORNER

Corn has long been a staple in the diet of folks from the Dark Corner. No crop has played a more dominant role in the survival of mountain people than the humble maize. For one thing, it can be grown almost anywhere, if it receives adequate sunlight and water. It will thrive on a hilly, rocky mountainside as well as in the dark, rich loam of a river bottom field. Plus, there's no crop more versatile. Few things bring more joy and pleasure to the heart of a countryman than picking the first few flavorsome ears of corn in early summer, shucking and boiling them immediately after harvest, then slathering them with rich, creamy farm-churned butter and liberally salting and peppering the golden bounty for a delicious, mouth-watering meal. What more could one possibly ask for?

The use of corn doesn't merely stop with the delightful "roastin' ear." Much of the corn grown in rural America is ground for animal feed. Without a doubt, though, the most vital role corn plays in country life is when it is mill-ground into cornmeal. Cornmeal is used for cornbread, the staff of life for generations of Dark Corner families. Cornbread is relatively simple to make, requiring few ingredients, and best of all, it really sticks to the ribs! Cornbread was often on the table three times a day out in the country. And though many a country cook baked biscuits daily for breakfast, there were often a few around the table who still preferred cornbread. Here is a popular recipe for old-timey Dark Corner cornbread.

DARK CORNER COUNTRY CORNBREAD

Preheat oven to 425 degrees
Grease an eight-inch iron skillet

In a bowl, combine:
1 egg
1 ½ cups self-rising cornmeal
2 cups buttermilk

Pour mixture into the skillet and cook for thirty minutes.

A pan of delicious country cornbread.

In addition to scrumptious cornbread being produced from cornmeal, we know that much of the meal ground in Dark Corner gristmills ended up in small, private distilleries that were scattered across hills and hollers. Moonshine couldn't be made without cornmeal.

So, corn really was the staff of life for so many a few generations back. Corn comes in two forms: yellow and white. For the most part, yellow corn is sweet corn. Over the years, it has been genetically engineered and modified to taste sweeter and sweeter. Today, certain varieties of hybrid yellow and bicolor corn are the favorites on tables across America. White corn, yellow corn's more homely country cousin, has traditionally been the variety used for cornmeal and animal feeds. But the old-timers out in the country will swear and declare white corn to be the all-out best for eating. They'll tell you that white corn is for people and yellow corn is for critters. It all seems to be a matter of taste, though.

It's been a long and winding journey for corn, from its earliest days of human cultivation, to becoming a basic staple in diets all across the world. It's estimated that corn, or maize, as it's also known, was first domesticated as a viable source of food by the Indigenous people of southern Mexico over 10,000 years ago. Around 2500 BC, it began its northward migration into America, brought here by Native Americans who were trading with their far-distant southern neighbors. Here, it was further developed through careful breeding, and it became more like the corn we're familiar with today.[36]

It is believed that early Spanish explorers were the first to introduce this remarkable grain to Europe, and soon it traveled from Spain and Portugal to southern France and Italy, where it became a popular ingredient in some Italian dishes. English settlers were later introduced to corn in Jamestown, Plymouth and other early North American colonies. These people soon learned about the amazing versatility of corn from their Native American neighbors. They learned, for example, that the hard, flinty kernel could be ground into a useful meal. The American Indians first ground their corn with a primitive mortar and pestle type of device fashioned from smooth stones that would be hollowed out for this purpose. The corn would be poured onto the stone and then pounded with another stone until the once hard kernel became a finely ground, powdery meal. The process of milling corn soon evolved.

Some of the earliest mills employed by white settlers to grind their corn were called tub mills. Easy to make and operate, the tub mill featured a horizontal water wheel contained in a wooden housing. Water was channeled to hit the horizontal wheel, which, in turn, rotated the millstones, thus grinding the grain slowly being fed into it. This process was laborious and inefficient, but early on, on the frontier, the tub mill prevailed.[37]

Refurbished mill wheel from Ballenger's Mill.

Later, the more sophisticated gristmill with the familiar vertical overshot wheel came on the scene. One critical requirement for the overshot wheel was a six-to-ten-foot constant fall of water. As the water struck the paddled spokes of the vertical mill wheel, a shaft inside the mill house would then

Ballenger's Mill built around 1820.

turn the millstones, which would then grind the corn that was being poured into a nearby hopper by the miller.

The first gristmill to operate in Greenville County was built sometime before 1776 by pioneer settler and Indian trader Richard Pearis. The mill was situated near the falls of the Reedy River in present-day downtown Greenville. Visitors to the falls today can well imagine the kind of power the swiftly moving waters of the river would have generated in running the mill. The mill was active until July 1776, when it was destroyed by a raiding band of Patriots under the command of Andrew Williamson. Pearis, a British sympathizer, raised the ire of his Whig neighbors, and he could only stand by and watch his home and mill go up in flames from the torch of the Patriot force.

After the American Revolution, and as more white settlers streamed into the foothills and mountains, more gristmills were built along the streams and rivers of the upstate. Not surprisingly, there were several of these early gristmills located in the Dark Corner. This was due, in part, to the acres of corn grown there, the amount of blockade whiskey distilled there and the rivers and streams that flow through there.

Earlier, we touched on the Alexander Lafayette Campbell Mill, connected in history with the historic and iconic Campbell Covered Bridge. Only the bridge remains today. The mill has been gone for many years, but it stood sentinel for a long time on a branch of the Middle Tyger River. Fate Campbell, its owner and operator, was a Confederate veteran who raised a large family close by.

The Fate Campbell Mill must not be confused with the other Dark Corner Campbell's Mill that was once owned by John Campbell. This mill was operating in 1880 and had a history reaching back all the way to 1805 when it was originally constructed by a man named Blassingame. Mann Batson stated, "In 1880 the mill was a $2,000.00 capital investment and had one employee who was paid one dollar a day. The mill had two stones and a maximum grinding capacity of twenty-five bushels a day. The height of the fall of the water was sixteen feet. The mill was open for business twelve hours per day May-November, and ten hours per day November-May."[38] This Campbell Mill was also powered by the waters of the Middle Tyger River.

One of the Dark Corner's oldest mills is still standing, but it hasn't been in operation for close to a century. Known now as Ballenger's Mill, it ground corn and wheat near a shoals of the Middle Tyger River, a millrace diverting the water onto the large, vertical upshot wheel.

Above: Interior of Ballenger's Mill.

Opposite: Manning Farmer. *Courtesy of Sandy Mason.*

The mill was constructed sometime around 1820 by Lewis H. Dickey, a wealthy planter who owned hundreds of acres around the Highland community. Dickey was also a slaveholder who, at one time, enslaved well over sixty Africans. The mill ground both corn and wheat. Lewis Dickey died in 1868, and the mill remained in the family for a short period of time before being sold.

It is assumed that it was at that point that it passed into the ownership of the Ballenger family.

Today Ballenger's Mill is on private property and is still in remarkably good shape considering that it's been standing for over two centuries. The mill wheel has been replaced in recent years, but when you step inside it's as if you've entered a time machine. The ancient mill stones are in place, and the massive wheels and cogs look as if they could begin turning at any time, though they couldn't. The huge, thick timbers, rough-hewn and sawed by raw manpower, are still rock solid, and they bear silent witness to the hard work and ingenuity of generations past.

A few enterprising residents of the Dark Corner in the past took it upon themselves, after the demise of water-powered gristmills in the area, to design their own corn grinding operations. The late Manning Farmer of the Ebenezer-Welcome community created his own electrically powered gristmill to grind his legendary Cocke's Prolific corn.

Cocke's Prolific was an early variety of flint corn developed by John Hartwell Cocke of Virginia in the very early 1800s. Cocke was a friend of Thomas Jefferson's, and it is believed that Jefferson may very well have grown this variety of corn at his Monticello estate. Cocke's Prolific, as it was called, was popular on farms across the South for generations, but close to a century ago it mysteriously disappeared from the scene. In fact, it was believed by many to have become extinct. This is where the Dark Corner Farmers come in. The Farmer family had been saving their seed from season to season. When their crop of Cocke's Prolific was harvested in the late summer, much of it would be ground for meal, some eaten in roasting ears, but always a generous portion would be safely stored away to be used as seed for the next growing season. Somehow, Professor David Shields of the University of South Carolina heard rumors that there was Cocke's Prolific being grown and saved up in the Dark Corner, so he made his way from Columbia to the Farmers' farm in Landrum. He collected some of the much sought-after seed, performed careful analysis of its genetics and confirmed that this corn was, indeed, the nearly extinct variety. Now Cocke's Prolific is widely available again after nearly a century of absence, and it's making its appearance in several different seed catalogues. And Manning Farmer's son Darrell is still faithfully growing the family corn in his late father's fallow fields, and then he grinds it, as his father did, into the delicious cornmeal that makes a delightful and flavorsome cake of golden cornbread.

Just a few miles from the Dark Corner in Greer one can still visit Suber's Corn Mill, one of the last remaining water-powered gristmills in the state of South Carolina. Jim and Linda Suber welcome visitors every Saturday to their family operation as they grind the delicious cornmeal their family has been known for three or four generations. They proudly sell their product on Saturdays down in Greer, and it's also available at retail outlets throughout the upstate. But up in the Dark Corner, there are no more corn mills operating as they did at one time. One can just imagine what it must have been like at Campbell's or Ballenger's as people brought their corn by the wagon load to be ground for their own personal consumption. Those were good and simple times, and they were golden, much like the golden-brown cakes of cornbread they produced.

12

THE HENSLEY BURNING

One of the most horrendous crimes ever committed in the Dark Corner remains an unsolved mystery to this very day. The so-called Hensley burning took place in the wee hours of the morning of April 9, 1893, on the side of Glassy Mountain as the home of Jane Hensley went up in flames, killing all four of its occupants: Jane, Esau, Silvania and Willis Hensley.

The Hensley home, an older log structure, was on the property of W.P. Hart, who employed the Hensleys as tenant farmers. The house was a well-known hangout for community rowdies. Wild parties were reported to be common there and were known to last all night. It was also a gambler's roost as well, and the ladies in residence there were of questionable character. It was rumored that members of some of the Dark Corner's finest families frequented the Hensley home from time to time.

When the flames started to dance across the midnight sky on Glassy's side, no one took notice because mountain wildfires were not at all that unusual in those days. Sometimes they were caused by lightning strikes. At other times, careless hunters left burning campfires that could easily be fanned out of control by high winds. And it was also not uncommon for farmers to rid their fields of weeds by burning them in the early spring. So, the first person who witnessed the flames would not have been especially concerned until they realized that it was, in fact, a house that was ablaze.

The burned embers were not discovered until the next day, about noon. James Moon happened upon the smoldering structure and, after further examination, was, no doubt, horrified to discover the charred remains of the

Hensley family. Others were summoned, and as they made their way through the ruins of the dwelling, they came upon the almost unrecognizable corpse of a man near the front door. Then, a woman, thought to be fifty-year old Jane, was found at another door. The body of the daughter, Silvania, was discovered in a bedroom, and the body of a young man, believed to be fourteen-year-old Willis, was discovered under the floorboards of the home. Immediately, foul play was suspected, because no one had escaped even though they were near doors and windows, which begged the question, Were they murdered before the fire was started?

John B. Dill was commissioned as a local magistrate the same year as the Hensley burning—1893. He served just three years, until 1896. Dill was an amiable storekeeper before he took the oath as magistrate. His country store was across from his comfortable white frame home, which was located at the intersection of the old Tugaloo and Dill Roads. His granddaughter, the late Ruth Thompson, lived in the old house for decades before her death, and I was her pastor from 1982 to 1984. When I visited her, she regaled me with stories about her legendary grandfather and some of the court decisions he had come to and the sentences he had meted out in his parlor/courtroom. I recall her pointing out a massive ancient oak across the road from her home and the stories she told of hangings in days gone by from the sturdy limbs of the old, gnarled tree. John B. Dill's home also served as a base of operations for federal revenue agents who would arrive there on Friday evenings. They would make plans for raiding stills the next day and spend the night there.

During his brief tenure as a magistrate, Judge Dill was often called on to act as coroner in murder inquests. Specifically, he presided over five such cases, including the Hensley burning.[39]

There was little useful evidence gained in this case. What was known was that the family of four included mother and grandmother Jane, who was fifty. Daughter Silvania was unmarried and aged twenty. Her brother Esau was twenty-four. And Jane's grandson Willis Hensley was fourteen. It was rumored that Silvania may have been pregnant at the time and the identity of the father was unknown.[40]

There was speculation that there had been a gathering of some sort at the home that night. What happened next remains a mystery. Was there some kind of confrontation about Sylvania's pregnancy? Was there a drunken brawl that resulted in a murder? Maybe it was a gambler's dispute that sparked the mayhem. What is known is a remark others had heard Willis make sometime before the fateful incident. The fourteen-year-old boy had undoubtedly witnessed some events in the home that frightened him

Only the fireplace remains from the home of magistrate John B. Dill, where so many Dark Corner inquests and trials took place, including the coroner's examination into the Hensley burning.

considerably. After one such event, Willis let it be known that the next time things got out of hand he was going to hide under the floorboards for safety. And that's exactly where they found his badly burned body.

An investigation of the tragedy proved inconclusive. A report in the *Greenville Mountaineer* from April 19, 1893, noted, "Nothing special was developed at the inquest, which was held by Trial Justice Dill, on Tuesday, April 11, and the jury rendered a verdict in accordance with the facts above given."

Of course, there was much speculation and gossip about the events of April 9 for years after that. Though it couldn't be proven, there were a group of fellows in the community who would have made credible suspects for the crime. They were known to have frequented the Hensley home, and the story goes that as the years passed these men stuck together in a most peculiar way. When one became deathly ill, the others gathered at his bedside to be sure the man made no incriminating death bed confessions. The strange behavior allegedly continued until the last of them was gone.[41]

There's one thing for certain: if anyone was indeed involved in this heinous crime, they took the mystery with them to the grave, and they left us with questions that most likely will never be answered.

13

A LIGHT IN THE DARK CORNER

In any detailed study of the Dark Corner, it's both easy and entertaining to dwell only on the sensational. The Greenville newspapers did this for years. The moonshine, the murders and the general mayhem that so often took place up there, after all, sold newspapers and piqued public curiosity. What seems to be lost in it all, though, is that most who know would agree that there is not to be found a higher concentration of devout, honest and down-to-earth folks than in that much maligned region called the Dark Corner.

Religion and faith have long played a prominent role in the life and culture of the Dark Corner. Faithful churches stand as living testimonies of generations that have made a real difference for the cause of Christianity. This influence reaches back a couple of centuries at least.

There is a common myth that the frontier of rural America has always been a stronghold of devout piety and morality. But in fact, nothing could be further from the truth. Early travelers into western territories in North Carolina, Tennessee and the upcountry of South Carolina often lamented the deplorable moral and spiritual conditions they found. The Methodist bishop of America Francis Asbury, who traveled widely for so many years across the western expanses of the frontier, frequently wrote in his journals about the drunkenness, sexual immorality and general biblical ignorance that he ran across daily in backwater settlements. This all gradually began to change with the arrival of a movement now known as the Second Great Awakening (1790–1840). While the First Great

Left: Foundation stone from the Original Head of Tyger Baptist Church. *Photo from* Tigerville: A Journey Through Time *by Geraldine Eppley and Candace Rathbone. Used by permission.*

Below: Tyger Baptist Church.

Awakening (1730–1760) was primarily a northeastern phenomenon, the Second Great Awakening was a revival movement that swept the southern frontier. Many of the Scots-Irish settlers who moved down the Great Wagon Road out of Philadelphia into the Carolinas brought with them some of the religious fervor that was spreading like a wildfire throughout Virginia and Kentucky. During these years, many of these people were moving into Greenville and Spartanburg Counties.

As the population grew, churches began to spring up here and there. Some of the earliest congregations to come along were Baptist and included Reedy

River Baptist, organized in 1778. Fork Shoals Baptist Church followed close behind in 1780. Then the first of the Dark Corner churches came to life. Head of Tyger Baptist Church (now Tyger Baptist Church), which was an arm, or mission of Reedy River, first appeared on record in 1793.

Brushy Creek Baptist Church in Taylors then came along in 1794. These four churches became the "mother" churches of most of the Greenville County Baptist congregations, and they were most prolific, which answers one of the first questions northerners ask when they come to this area, "Why are there so many Baptist churches down here?"

On July 16, 1809, a group of believers began meeting at a crossroads one mile west of the village of Gowensville. It wasn't until May 5, 1820, that the church officially constituted and became known, most appropriately, as Crossroads Baptist Church, still another offspring of Head of Tyger Baptist Church. In 1847, the man who created the wildly popular hymnal known as *Southern Harmony* was conducting a shaped note singing school at Crossroads. William Walker, a native of Union County, was well-known and beloved across much of the South. He was the first person to popularize John Newton's classic hymn "Amazing Grace." The song had pretty much been lost to obscurity until 1835, when Walker changed the title of the hymn from "Faith's Review and Expectation" to "Amazing Grace." He also gave it a hauntingly beautiful new tune that we still enjoy to this day. As he conducted that meeting for the people of Crossroads, he couldn't believe that the strong, growing congregation was limited to such a small, cramped facility. He owned a five-acre tract of land on a beautiful hillside one mile east of the church in Gowensville, and he graciously gave that land to the church as a gift. And by the following year, Crossroads had built a new, spacious church building on the hillside with a commanding view of the mountains. The church changed its name to Gowensville Baptist Church in 1873. In addition to its picture postcard appearance, Gowensville Baptist Church has one of the most historic cemeteries in the area. A lot can be learned about local history by wandering among the tombstones and reading the family names that once were so prominent here.

Liberty Methodist Church, just off State Highway 14, and on State Highway 414, is one of the oldest Methodist congregations in the upstate. There's not a lot of recorded history available on Liberty, but we do know it was organized on November 10, 1832. There is speculation that the church resulted from a camp meeting that was taking place that year on Bird Mountain, just outside Tryon, North Carolina. Evangelistic camp meetings were often a part of what we referred to earlier as the Second

Top: Gowensville Baptist Church.

Bottom: Liberty United Methodist Church.

Top: Glassy Mountain Baptist Church.

Bottom: Highland Baptist Church.

Great Awakening. Liberty has long been an important part of Methodist faith and tradition in this area. There is also an oral tradition, yet unproven, that Liberty may have played a role in the attempt locally to free slaves. Some think it may even be possible that enslaved Africans were channeled to the Underground Railroad from Liberty, but again, that's merely speculation.

In 1833, the Head of Tyger Baptist Church once again established another mission that would come to be known as Glassy Mountain Baptist Church. And it is well-named because it does, indeed, stand in the shadow of the great mountain. This is a historic church, partly because, early on, it was a gathering place for political rallies and community events. It was here at Glassy Mountain that Governor Benjamin Perry presented his theory on the naming of the Dark Corner. Like Gowensville, Glassy Mountain also has an old and historic cemetery, and many of the mossy headstones tell graphic and detailed stories of those buried there.

Other prominent Dark Corner churches include Highland Baptist Church, which began life as a Methodist church called Dickey Chapel. Named for Lewis H. Dickey, who donated the property for the church, it was later sold to a Baptist group and eventually became known as Highland. In the Highland cemetery rests several important members of the Dark Corner community, including Reverend A.D. Bowers, pioneer Baptist preacher who founded several local Baptist churches. Also buried here is Dr. James A. Howard, the Baptist preacher turned Dark Corner historian who wrote *Dark Corner Heritage*, which was really the first historical record of the Dark Corner. One of the oldest, if not the oldest grave in the Highland cemetery belongs to Jacob Kytle, buried there in 1843. He was a soldier in the American Revolution and a pioneer settler of the Dark Corner.

Later additions to the Dark Corner's church landscape include Ebenezer-Welcome Baptist Church, organized in 1878 by Reverend A.D. Bowers. The hyphenated name of the church came as a result of members of the church family worrying that their congregation might be confused with the much older Ebenezer Baptist Church located over in Travelers Rest. And so, the word *Welcome* was added with a hyphen, and the problem was solved. Buried in the Ebenezer-Welcome cemetery are such Dark Corner personalities as James Lafayette Campbell, the Civil War veteran for whom the Campbell Covered Bridge was named, and James Alexander Campbell, otherwise known as "Big Alec."

Not only have churches had a profound effect for good on the Dark Corner community, but there have also been some other important institutions that have left their mark as well.

Right: Grave marker of Revolutionary War veteran Jacob Kytle. One of the earliest graves in the Highland Baptist Church cemetery.

Below: Ebenezer-Welcome Baptist Church.

North Greenville University, located in the Tigerville community, is now well-known as a world-class institution of higher learning, offering advanced degrees in everything from traditional education to physician's assistant's training. This now prestigious school started life with humble beginnings. Founded in 1891, its inception was spearheaded by the North Greenville Baptist Association for the education of local youth.

Known first as North Greenville Academy, the school offered only the most basic high school level education. In 1934, in addition to its high school curriculum, North Greenville began offering a two-year junior college degree. In 1992, the college became fully accredited and established a four-year bachelor's degree program. It earned university status in 2006 and is still known, according to its motto, as the school where "Christ makes the difference."

Christian education was also near and dear to the heart of another Dark Corner resident by the name of Thomas J. Earle. Earle lived in the Gowensville community and was part of a prominent upstate pioneer family with roots in Virginia. The family migrated to the northern part of Greenville County early on. After graduation from Georgia's Mercer University, Thomas J. Earle returned to the area, where he began a long and distinguished career as a much beloved Baptist minister. His longest tenure at a church was actually at the Gowensville Baptist Church, where he served with distinction from 1856 until his death in 1889. Early in his ministry, Earle was especially troubled by the lack of educational opportunities for local youth. Ignorance flourished in the Dark Corner and surrounding areas, and Earle and others were unhappy about it. As a result, he opened what would come to be known as the Earle Seminary in Gowensville in 1858. The school was an immediate success and was well received by all. The academy drew students, not just from the local area, but in regions beyond, from as far away as Georgia and North Carolina. This prompted the need for boarding facilities for the students. Not only were some local families willing to offer bed and board, but Reverend Earle was as well.

Earle's lovely home is still standing just off State Highway 14, about one mile north of Gowensville. It's an imposing two-story structure, made of dark, red brick, and resembling an antebellum plantation house. Today it's occupied by members of the same family who have lived

North Greenville University. Founded in 1891 as North Greenville Academy.

Earlesdale, the home of Reverend Thomas J. Earle. *Courtesy of Jimmie Lynn Dykes.*

there for two or three generations. It still bears the name Earlesdale in honor of its original owner.

The tale goes, though it may be apocryphal, that the second story of the Earle home was dedicated to dormitory space for the boarding students of the seminary. To separate the boys from the girls, Reverend Earle allegedly raised a partition down the middle of the second story hallway. It wasn't long, though, before the enterprising boys and girls learned they could meet out on the rooftop.

Students at the Earle Seminary received a classical education that included advanced courses in Latin, Greek, literature and mathematics. School records indicate that the academy, not surprisingly, experienced some lean times during the Civil War years but soon thereafter revived and thrived. In 1869, the school's official enrollment was fifty-five.

Earle Seminary remained open until shortly after Reverend Earle's death in 1889. Many believe Earle's passing and the subsequent closing of the school prompted the North Greenville Baptist Association to open the North Greenville Academy in 1891 to address the loss of this beloved and valued institution of learning. Thomas J. Earle is buried in the Gowensville Baptist Church cemetery, and his tall obelisk monument bears witness to the affection and high esteem with which he was held by every congregation he served.

These churches and institutions, along with others that could certainly be mentioned, have cast a long shadow for good over the Dark Corner, and many have been positively affected by their influence. And they continue to make a positive and profound impact to this very day.

14

TROUBLE IN A JUG

Unfortunately, when most folks think of the Dark Corner, the first thing that comes to mind is moonshine whiskey. That is unfortunate because there are so many other wonderful dimensions to this beautiful and historic corner of Greenville County. Blockade whiskey is just a small part of the story. Nevertheless, it is a story that probably needs to be told. Dr. Jim Howard estimated that between 1900 and 1924, there were at least fourteen killings in the Dark Corner related to the making and the consumption of bootleg whiskey.[42] While it is true that several Dark Corner families were supported by the manufacture of moonshine, it's also true that just as many, if not more, families were devastated by its consumption and the want and heartache that it caused.

The long-standing practice of distilling whiskey reaches far back in time, long before the settlement of the Dark Corner. Early pioneers brought their family recipes with them from the British Isles. When the Scots and northern Englishmen were sent by the English king to Northern Ireland to help in subduing the Irish revolutionaries, they learned the technique of whiskey making from those same Irishmen they were living among. Of course, the Scotsmen already had a long and colorful history of whiskey making before they ever moved to Ireland. It was from these experiences that they both learned and then transported those same techniques with them to the American colonies. This know-how, however, was not always welcomed or encouraged on American soil.

In 1791, Secretary of the Treasury Alexander Hamilton levied an excise tax on whiskey, and with that tax came strict enforcement of the law. And so began the long, historic struggle between the distiller and the revenue officer. In 1794, a veritable war broke out in western Pennsylvania between the administration of President George Washington and the Scots-Irish settlers, who were willing to fight to the death for, what they believed, was their God-given right to distill their own spirits without government interference or intervention. The so-called Whiskey Rebellion ended only when Washington sent a militia ten thousand strong to arrest the ringleaders of the insurrection. And yet, as these same Scots-Irish settlers continued to move south down the Great Wagon Road into the Carolinas, Tennessee and Georgia, they continued to build their stills, distill their spirits and defend to the death their right to do so.

Dark Corner jug.

Whiskey making in the Dark Corner after the Civil War was so common and widespread that it has been reported that local streams were so polluted and choked by distillery waste that it was even impossible for livestock to drink safely. The thick woods and hidden coves of the area proved to be perfect hideouts for the stealthy moonshiner.

Corn whiskey was relatively simple to make and required few ingredients, but there was a fairly detailed and complex procedure one had to follow to make it safely and successfully. In the Sunday, February 12, 1967 edition of the *Greenville News*, there was a section of the paper dedicated to telling the story of the Dark Corner. Ninety-two-year-old William Center, a native of the Dark Corner, was interviewed on the subject of old-time moonshine making. He gave the following detailed account:

> *First, you got the corn which you shucked and shelled out and took to the mill and had it ground. White or yellow corn would do equally well. You had a hogshead over a fire and when the water began to boil you emptied*

about a bushel and a half of the meal in it. It took about twenty-five gallons of water, and you stirred it a long time with a mash stick. It cooked up almost like cornbread. Then you covered it over until the next day. You put malt or yeast into it—the storekeeper always kept in on hand—it was sprouted barley usually and took five or six pounds a batch. It began to work—ferment—and you let it work for about two days. Then it was ready for you to dip it up and put it into your still. According to Mr. Center, it took about an hour and a half to run one batch through the "cap and worm" of the still. The still was usually made of copper and was set on a large, flat stone under which a fire had been kindled. In order to get a sufficiently high temperature to make the mash evaporate for distillation it was necessary to build a stone oven around the still to keep the heat in. That made the purest whiskey that could be made. There wasn't any vardi grease at all. Mr. Center said, as he explained how the distilled liquid was allowed to run into a funnel filled with charcoal and thence into a wooden keg. You could drink it right then, he said, but the whiskey got a better and softer taste if it was allowed to age in the wood. Whiskey won't age in a glass or crockery container, it has to be in wood, he stressed.

When the job of the moonshiner was done, the job of the bootlegger had just begun. The moonshiner was the maker, and the bootlegger was the distributor. Improved roads and the advent of the automobile opened up all kinds of marketing opportunities for the enterprising whiskey maker. Now moonshine could easily and quickly be transported to cities and towns to accommodate a new kind of thirsty consumer. The Prohibition years made it even more profitable for these entrepreneurs of the hills.

Old-fashioned moonshine still. *Courtesy of Don Brown.*

Of course, the sworn enemy of every moonshiner was the despised revenue officer, simply known as the "revenuer." All kinds of entertaining, and sometimes, half-true stories exist about the cat-and-mouse games that were played between the speedy and wily bootlegger and the equally determined law enforcement officer. Oftentimes, the bootlegger installed a souped-up, oversized engine in his smaller car that would enable him to outrun just about any revenue agent around. Heavy-duty rear-end springs in his automobile also permitted him to pack his trunk with case after case of blockade whiskey without weighing the back of his car down and giving away the presence of his hefty payload. The roots of NASCAR go back to the days of these swift bootleggers who finally channeled their need for speed into good and started competing against each other in legal races on paved racetracks.

Generally speaking, though, there was a healthy and mutual respect that existed between the moonshiner, bootlegger and the law enforcement officer. Longtime Greenville County sheriff P.D. Gilreath, who administered justice in the county in the late nineteenth and early twentieth centuries, rarely even carried a gun, and he prosecuted just as many criminals as anyone. He did this because he knew and respected the people and the culture of upper Greenville County. While he would hold people responsible for their crimes, he treated them and their families with kindness and respected their property rights. At times, this even got the genial sheriff in trouble himself with higher authorities, especially the hot-tempered governor of South Carolina Benjamin "Pitchfork" Tillman, who served as governor from 1890 to 1894 and later became the U.S. senator from South Carolina. In December 1892, Tillman created the South Carolina Dispensary, intended to be the only legal outlet for alcoholic beverages in the state of South Carolina. Tillman was intent on putting all other manufacturers of liquor in the state out of business, and he prosecuted violators to the fullest extent of the law. And in the process, he wasn't above ignoring the personal and constitutional rights of those whom he pursued and prosecuted. In addition, he expected all law enforcement officers of the state to follow suit. Sheriff Gilreath's refusal to arrest a Greenville County resident named Edel—who was, in fact, in violation of state dispensary laws—because his wife was "in a delicate state" almost cost the sheriff his job, but in the process, he endeared himself even more to the residents of Greenville County.[43] It was not at all uncommon for Gilreath to allow accused moonshiners to take care of personal business before being jailed. He would inform them of when they needed to appear before the magistrate, and usually they would arrive on time to hear their sentence. There were times when the good sheriff had egg on his face. You may recall that it was Sheriff Gilreath who allowed Little Bill Howard's wife to visit him in jail, only to have Little Bill escape in his wife's dress and bonnet.

Jim "Tank" Tankersley, a resident of the River Falls community and a federal revenue officer until his retirement in 1977, had a similar relationship with the whiskey makers of upper Greenville County. Hired as an agent in 1952, he vigorously pursued those who were breaking the law, but he also understood the challenges and tough circumstances many of these people faced in life. In 1980, Tankersley sat down with writer Jerry Bledsoe and reflected on some of the experiences he had while serving as a revenuer. He described some of the sympathetic feelings he had for those folks he often pursued so relentlessly. "You'd try to get 'em in jail, and then you'd try to get 'em out. Feel sorry for 'em, go down and talk to the judge."[44] And these same people would sometimes return the favor. Tankersley recollected about the time he was seriously injured in an automobile accident while chasing a bootlegger near Greenville. He remembered that the hallways of the old Greenville hospital were crowded with moonshiners who had come to pay their respects to his wife and even offer financial assistance to the family. He never forgot that.[45]

Despite such records of friendliness and cordiality, make no mistake about it, moonshiners and bootleggers alike still faced a stiff penalty for their crimes. Especially those who were repeat offenders. Oftentimes a man in the Dark Corner would disappear for a year or two, and there would be few questions from family and neighbors about their whereabouts. Most knew the missing person was serving a sentence in the federal penitentiary in Atlanta and that after a time they would return home.

Even today, there are those hardy souls among us who still tempt fate by taking to the woods with all the necessary ingredients to "make a turn" of whiskey. And so, on a much smaller scale, the battle and the trouble continue even to this day.

15

A DARK CORNER HERO

In his 1914 autobiography *A Mountain Boy's Life Story*, Dean Crain wrote of the role fearless country preachers played in the history and spiritual formations of the Dark Corner. He said, "It will take all eternity to know the good the pioneer preachers have done in the mountains. They fearlessly traveled every hog path in the mountains of Greenville County. They warned faithfully the moonshiners, and they were not deterred by the threats of these lawless men." Then Crain named one such preacher. He said, "Rev. A.D. Bowers was a hero in the Dark Corner for the gospel's sake."[46]

The word *hero* is an ambitious term to use in describing a simple country preacher, and I'm sure it's one A.D. Bowers never would have used to describe himself. And yet, when you think of the message he preached and the opposition he routinely faced, one would have to agree with Crain that it took heroic courage and sheer tenacity to consistently stand for what he stood for and to stand against that which he opposed. This was particularly true when it came to the making of blockade whiskey. Bowers consistently condemned this practice, and in the process, he raised the ire of a lot of people who made their living at a still.

Reverend Alex D. Bowers was a native of the Dark Corner. He was born on February 22, 1826, in the upper part of Greenville County, and his parents owned a small farm and made their living as subsistence farmers, as did most Dark Corner residents back in those days. Little is known about Bowers's family or childhood. Also unknown is his age at conversion. We do know he was licensed to preach by Glassy Mountain Baptist Church in 1859

Reverend A.D. Bowers. *Courtesy of ancestry.com.*

and was subsequently ordained for ministry by the church two years later in 1861. In those days, Glassy Mountain Baptist Church cast a long shadow upon the spiritual landscape of the Dark Corner. For many years, the church was led quite capably and faithfully by the longtime pastor Elder Jesse Center. Center, a native Englishman, moved to the Dark Corner of Greenville County when it was sparsely settled. He homesteaded in the area of Glassy Mountain and soon became the church's second pastor. Undoubtedly, he was a powerful influence on young Bowers and became his mentor, helping to prepare him for his long and successful ministry.

The same year Alex Bowers was ordained at Glassy Mountain, South Carolina seceded from the Union, and a long, bloody civil war ensued. Bowers volunteered for the Confederate army, and he faithfully served the cause, later being honorably discharged. After the war, he launched his ministry in earnest—a ministry that would prove to be lengthy and productive. During that ministry, he served twenty-three churches. And he was personally responsible for organizing six of those twenty-three. He started Oak Grove Baptist Church in the community where he had lived for most of his life. He also organized Locust Hill, Highland, Camp Creek, Ebenezer-Welcome and Reedy River Cotton Mill Church. At the same time, he was active in the North Greenville Baptist Association, where he served a term as moderator.

One thing A.D. Bowers is most remembered for was his strong and uncompromising stand against the manufacture and consumption of alcohol. The temperance movement, especially among Southern Baptists, really began gaining momentum after the Civil War. This may be partly so because of the astonishing rise of alcohol consumption among returning veterans. So many soldiers in that war, on both sides, saw and personally experienced such horrific conditions that alcohol became a way for them to escape the memories that haunted them constantly. The results on the individuals and their families were devastating. Bowers, a veteran himself, saw the damaging effects that readily available homemade whiskey was having on Dark Corner residents. As a result, he took a strong stand and preached a gospel of total abstinence unswervingly. This dedication nearly cost him his life on a few occasions.

There's one famous account that underlines the preacher's courage and commitment. Bowers was receiving death threats on a regular basis because of his pointed preaching, but he was undeterred. One Sunday, as he was preaching, the story goes that some local rowdies showed up at the church with the intention of killing the preacher. As Bowers was holding forth, they nudged their rifle barrels through the open window of the church and took aim at the fearless pastor. Bowers stopped his sermon in mid-sentence and addressed his would-be assassins at the window, saying, "God has given me this sermon to preach, and I intend to finish it. You fellers can kill me when I'm done."

Then he took up where he left off and preached a long and powerful Bible message. Evidently, the potential killers were so affected by the courage and resolve of the preacher they withdrew their rifles from the window and returned to their homes without accomplishing their mission.

Another tale is told of the boldness of Bowers. Supposedly, a band of Mormon missionaries was moving through the upper part of Greenville County and camping somewhere around the Highland community with the intention of spending a day or two proselytizing to the local Baptists and Methodists. When Reverend Bowers caught wind of their mission, he went to where they were camping and introduced himself. Then he told them, "If y'all ain't out of this community by tomorrow we'll set some folks on you!"

The Mormons must have been convinced the country parson meant business because they soon struck camp and headed for safer places.

For forty-eight years, Reverend Alex D. Bowers faithfully ministered to the people of the upper part of Greenville County, and as the story goes, he never received pay for his services. Dr. James Howard gives an account in *Dark Corner Heritage* of being present for one of Bowers's last sermons. He recalled, "The last sermon the writer heard Alex D. Bowers preach, the old preacher was so feeble that he sat in a chair and preached with deep compassion and with tears, on the subject: 'Mary Hath Chosen That Good Part.'"[47]

And though the reverend was sick and infirmed by age, Howard recalled that all present were deeply moved by his sincere delivery. Reverend A.D. Bowers died at the age of eighty-three on February 2, 1909. Both he and his wife are buried in the Highland Baptist Church cemetery. The North Greenville Baptist Association, at its annual meeting in 1909, entered the following tribute to Bowers in the associational minutes:

> *Born in Greenville County, S.C. February 22, 1826 and was married to Mary Center in 1846. Was granted a license to preach by Glassy Mountain Baptist Church July 2, 1859. Was ordained July 10, 1861. He was pastor of twenty-three churches. He organized Oak Grove, Locust Hill, Highland, Camp Creek, Ebenezer-Welcome, and Reedy River Cotton Mill Church. He was moderator of the North Greenville Baptist Association 1893–1894. Died February 2, 1909.*[48]

Reverend A.D. Bowers would be affectionately remembered for years to come, and perhaps his greatest contributions to the religious life of the Dark Corner are the churches he organized that continue to faithfully serve God and the communities they are in.

16

DICKEY'S PLANTATION

One of the largest and most productive antebellum plantations in the upstate of South Carolina was in the Dark Corner of Greenville County, and any uninformed motorist who might pass by its former location would never guess the flurry of activity that was taking place there 165 years ago. I am, of course, speaking of the large estate and home of Lewis H. Dickey, which was comfortably situated near the modern-day intersection of States Highways 101 and 414. Turning off Highway 101 on to 414, going toward Greer, the large plantation house would have been found on the vacant land to the right-hand side of the road. Today, it's merely a tangle of vines and overgrown trees, but then it was a magnificent home. In addition to being a beautiful residence, it also served as the headquarters for a busy and prosperous farming operation.

Lewis Dickey, the son of a prominent Revolutionary War veteran, was a native of Rutherford County, North Carolina. What would have brought him to the Dark Corner is anyone's guess. He may have been intrigued by the wide availability of large tracts of land at reasonable prices that existed at that time. Records indicate that Dickey began acquiring property in the area in 1824. His first acquisition was a tract of 740 acres that he purchased on the "Sink Hole of the Middle Tyger River."[49] By 1860 (just eight years before his death), he had accumulated well over 2,000 acres in the vicinity; 700 acres of this land was classified as "improved," which was a way of saying this land was arable and was being farmed with profit. Lewis Dickey also bore the dubious distinction of being one of the largest slaveholders in Greenville County. In 1864, he held sixty-four enslaved Africans on his vast estate. Around 1824, Dickey constructed a gristmill on a shoal of the Middle Tyger River, just north of his home. This was a busy, moneymaking operation for the enterprising Dickey. In 1850, Dickey's Mill processed five thousand bushels of cornmeal. The milling was overseen by one of Dickey's slaves. This gristmill later passed out of the ownership of the Dickey family and eventually came to be known as Ballenger's Mill, which operated well into the twentieth century. Though long abandoned, the mill house is still standing today. It's located on private property and is not accessible to the general public. But the fact that the old mill is still standing after two centuries is a testimony to the skill and ingenuity of its original builders.

Up to just a few years ago, the Dickey house was still standing, though in a state of great neglect and disrepair. When Lewis Dickey chose the location for his home in the 1820s, he knew, as modern realtors and homeowners know, it's all about location. The intersection of current State Highways 101 and 414 was once the confluence of two major roads that passed through upper Greenville County. The Saluda Gap Road (part of which is now Highway 101) proceeded out of the mountains of western North Carolina and through the Saluda Gap. It was also known as the Turnpike, or the Toll Road, and it was an important highway, not only for travelers but also for farmers who were bringing their products and livestock from their farms in the mountains to the markets of South Carolina and Georgia. So, the Saluda Gap Road daily carried a lot of traffic right past the Dickey plantation. And then the other major road passing by Dickey's was the old Tugaloo Road (part of which is now Highway 414). Originally an ancient warrior's path, the road was eventually claimed by early settlers who traveled it all the way from Virginia to the Tugaloo River on the Georgia–South Carolina border. In fact, just north and adjacent to Highway 414 is a stretch of country road that is still called Tugaloo Road, and it is believed that this is the only part of the old road that still bears the Tugaloo name.

Lewis Dickey, being the entrepreneur he was, took full advantage of the high volume of traffic generated by these two roads and built a store, blacksmith shop and some other commercial enterprises close by to capitalize on the constant flow of travelers. The old Highland post office was in Dickey's store, and he was its first postmaster. He served in this position from 1843 to 1866. Up to just a few years ago, there had been small stores at this same location since Dickey first built his there in the 1820s.

Dickey's home across the way was a showcase in those early days, admired by all who passed that way. Generations ago, the Chester newspaper offered a detailed description of this magnificent home:

> *It is two stories in height, and definitely built in two sections, and a back wing of one story. It is built of wood on a rock foundation, and once had a full cellar, now partially bricked up. It was heated by huge fireplaces. Interior rooms have wide plank floors and walls and baseboards and mantles are painted to resemble dark marble. Some doors still have huge locks but there are no keys. It could once be completely shut off from the outside with solid doors and window shutters. Portholes may be seen from upstairs rooms, near the chimneys, through which, the story goes, shots were fired at Yankee soldiers during the Civil War. In all probability, the house was built by Lewis H. Dickey. It seems logical to think the house was erected shortly after 1824 when the land was acquired.*

In addition to the home, store, post office and blacksmith shop, there were other notable activities that took place around Highland Grove in those early days. The local militia was known to meet for training and drilling at Dickey's plantation. Military musters were required to be held regularly in order to train local soldiers in the event of a crisis, such as a slave uprising. But these meetings evolved into social gatherings for the entire community. Political speeches were made, barbecues were hosted and there were usually competitive horse races. In fact, it has been reported that Dickey had a racetrack on his property as well. So, Dickey's crossroads became an important gathering spot for the folks of the upper part, and it was well known.

And since the spiritual and religious life of the community was of such great value, Lewis Dickey built a small Methodist chapel on his property to accommodate local worshippers. It wasn't far at all from his home. The church was appropriately named Dickey's Chapel, and soon it included a plot of land for a community burial ground. As one wanders through the cemetery there, one might be struck by the number of worn and weathered gravestones that tell the story of several generations of families being laid to rest there. Dickey's wife, Mary, is buried there, as are several other members of the Dickey family. Oddly enough, though, the grave of Lewis Dickey is not to be found in the churchyard. In fact, no one knows where the once wealthy planter was laid to rest. The speculation is that he is either in an unmarked grave in the church cemetery or perhaps he was buried somewhere closer to his home. It remains a Dark Corner mystery.

In 1896, the small Methodist group that occupied Dickey's Chapel sold the church to a group of Baptists for $105. The Baptists changed the name of the church to Wilson Grove Baptist Church in honor of the Wilson family who, at that time, owned the property. A little later, the name was changed once again to Highland Baptist Church, and the name remains to this day.

As mentioned earlier, after Lewis Dickey's death in 1868, his home was purchased by the Wilson family, and members of that family occupied the property for several years thereafter. After it passed from the hands of the Wilsons, the home and surrounding property soon fell into a state of neglect, and it didn't take long for nature to reclaim this once beautiful and well-tended estate. Soon the badly dilapidated house had to be razed, and now little if anything remains that would remind passersby of the stately home's former glory.

As one would expect, all kinds of legends and strange tales have emerged over the years involving the abandoned house and property. Tales of hauntings and eerie phenomena have become common around those parts. It is claimed by some—though, it would be hard to substantiate nearly two hundred years later—that Lewis Dickey was especially cruel to the people he enslaved on his plantation, and he often beat them mercilessly for little if any reason. The dark legend has it that he would take the unfortunate victim down to the cellar of his home and there he would chain him or her to a beam and cruelly whip them while they were manacled. And so the story goes, if you pass close by to the ruins of the plantation house late at night, you're liable to hear the rattle of chains and the pained moans of the victim being tortured.

The other story, also unsubstantiated, claims that the cruel, ruthless Dickey was in the practice of robbing and killing hapless strangers who were lodging near his place at night. It wasn't uncommon for Dickey to take in travelers who were coming from North Carolina down the Saluda Gap Road or the Tugaloo Road. Legend has it that after robbing and murdering his guests, he cast their bodies down into an abandoned well on the back of his property. So, in addition to the rattling chains one might hear at night, there were also the blood-curdling screams of those who were thrown into a deep, dark well. Most likely, there's little if any truth to either one of these urban legends, but it makes for good late-night storytelling, especially around a flickering campfire just up the road at Camp Old Indian, the nearby Boy Scout camp.

17

SHOOTOUT AT MOUNTAIN HILL CHURCH

Old-time mountain feuds often began over the pettiest disagreements or some kind of minor squabble. But then they could escalate very quickly, especially if you add a nip or two of strong corn whiskey. And these disagreements almost always never ended well. The Dark Corner has witnessed its share of these kinds of conflicts, but none was bloodier or more dramatic than the infamous shootout at Mountain Hill Baptist Church that took place on Sunday morning, August 23, 1891. Worshipers who arrived at church on that sultry August morning could never have guessed what they were about to witness.

Mountain Hill Baptist Church was formed in 1869, and for the most part, its membership was composed of people who lived either on or around Glassy Mountain. The church sits high atop Glassy in a serene, peaceful location that is particularly well-suited for worship, prayer and meditation. The church remains at that spot to this very day, albeit in a lovely, modern building. Nowadays the church and ancient cemetery are isolated from the rest of the world by the carefully guarded gates of the Cliffs at Glassy community.

In 1891, the existing rustic church building served not only as a place of community worship, but during the week the structure served double duty as a community schoolhouse as well.

It was communion Sunday at Mountain Hill on that fateful morning, and church member Richard Gosnell was walking into the sanctuary with a bottle of wine that was to be used for the Lord's supper. He was stopped in

Mountain Hill Baptist Church high atop Glassy Mountain.

his tracks by a surly Joshua Howard, who snarled at Gosnell and said, "Do you mean to slight me, and mean it as an insult?" Accompanying Howard that morning were his brothers Massena, Dick and Tom. Joshua Howard and his brother Massena were no strangers to trouble. At the time of this Mountain Hill clash, Joshua was under a bench warrant for a previous charge of carrying a concealed weapon. And at the same time, he was wanted up in North Carolina for breaking out of jail after he was arrested for rioting. In 1888, his brother Massena was seriously wounded by a pistol shot from someone who believed he was reporting his still. So, the Howards had already been in their fair share of scrapes and brushes with the law, and they were both disasters waiting to happen. And that disaster was about to happen on this peaceful Sunday morning.

Richard Gosnell ignored Josh Howard's threatening and inflammatory remarks and continued to walk into the church. This further infuriated Howard, and at this point he withdrew a revolver and began shooting wildly in Gosnell's direction. Then everything rapidly fell apart. A veritable battle ensued outside the church as comrades from both parties got involved and started firing their weapons. It was estimated that there were forty to fifty shots fired in the span of just a minute or so. Massena Howard was the first hit, by a shot to the abdomen, and he died almost immediately. Joshua Howard was shot in the back and lived until the next day. Dick Howard was slightly wounded and survived. Luther Durham, a friend of Gosnell's, was shot in the stomach and the mouth, but he also survived. Thomas Howard took a glancing blow to the head and lived. Sherman Bridgeman, another friend of Richard Gosnell's, was also wounded by a shot to the head.

The entire tragic event was over in a matter of seconds, and in the flurry of gunfire, no doubt, potential witnesses were sent scattering across the church grounds seeking cover. Because of this, witness testimony was sketchy. What was summarized in the coroner's inquest that took place just two days later was that Sherman Bridgeman was responsible for the death of Joshua Howard with C.A. Gosnell and Rufus Durham as accessories to his murder. Dina Howard, the wife of Massena Howard, implicated Rufus Durham in her husband's killing. She testified that she ran to her husband as he was dying, and he told her that Rufus "Babe" Durham pulled the trigger of the gun that felled him.[50]

The ones indicted by the coroner's jury would not stand trial until November. They had the good fortune of being defended by J. Alender Mooney, one of Greenville's most prominent and successful attorneys. Mooney was also a native of the Dark Corner, having been born and raised in the Gowensville community. Mooney's father was the much beloved Dark Corner physician William A. Mooney, who spent his life doctoring area residents, charging little, if anything, for his services. Dr. Mooney also, at one time, served in the South Carolina House of Representatives. Ironically, Dr. Mooney was present at Mountain Hill that morning, though he was a longtime member of Gowensville Baptist Church. He was also a witness at the coroner's inquest. Partly because of Alender Mooney's expert defense of his clients, along with the convoluted and confusing testimony of the witnesses to the event, all parties were acquitted of the Howard brothers' murders.

The real motivation for Howard's actions in the first place is still veiled in mystery and may never be known. At one time, Joshua Howard worked for the Durhams, and something involving that experience may have very well played a role in his actions. Were the Durhams, Gosnell and Bridgeman expecting trouble that day? Apparently, all the reinforcements had been called in, and they were armed to the teeth. There's one thing for sure, though. Most who came to Mountain Hill Baptist Church to worship on that peaceful August Sunday morning had no idea that their quiet Sabbath would be violently disrupted by gunfire, mayhem and murder.

Author Margaret Morley, in her timeless classic, *The Carolina Mountains*, has an interesting footnote to this infamous event in her book. Morley, a resident of Tryon, traveled one Sunday across the mountain and came upon Mountain Hill Baptist Church. She records,

> *The road leads to an unpainted church on top of the mountain where on "preaching-day" the women assemble in their best black sunbonnets and the men in their Sunday clothes. From the lonely little "church house" a path guides you to the top of Glassy Rock, whose steep front shines like glass when wet-which is much of the time. As we sit here one day, a mountaineer approaches, and, pointing to a man crossing a field on muleback far below, laconically remarks, "That gentleman's pa was killed at Glassy Mountain church." Then he tells how the people were waiting for the preacher to come one Sunday, when suddenly shots were heard, and two men of the congregation fell dead. The cause of this ghastly deed was the usual one, a quarrel between two moonshiners; and the method of revenge was characteristic, one of the men having warned the other that if he went to church next preaching-day, he would have him arrested. Of course, he went.*[51]

Margaret Morley probably got this information from the man with whom she was speaking and so the motivation for murder appears to be a moonshiner's feud: the unforgiveable sin of one moonshiner reporting another.

Interestingly, there were more gunshots fired at Mountain Hill Baptist Church on that fateful Sunday morning in 1891 than there were fired at the OK Corral in Tombstone, Arizona, on March 26, 1881. Forty to fifty shots rang out at Mountain Hill, with the result being two deaths, while an estimated thirty rounds were fired at the OK Corral with three killed. The shooting at Mountain Hill did little to improve the Dark Corner's image to the outside world. It seemed as if in those days there was no safe haven up there, not even in the House of God.

18

FUNERALS IN THE DARK CORNER

Every civilization down through the centuries has shared one thing in common, and that is the desire and the need to bury their dead with honor and dignity. In this tradition, the folks up in the Dark Corner, from the time of its earliest settlement, have been faithful in honoring loved ones who have gone before them, though, granted, funeral practices and traditions have changed dramatically over the years.

In the days before funeral homes and morticians were commonplace, families took it upon themselves to bury their loved ones from start to finish. Upon the announcement of a death in the community friends and family would get busy and attend to the final needs of the departed. They would bathe the body of the deceased, dress him or her in their finest clothes and position the body on a bed for everyone to view as they came to pay respects to the family. In the meantime, community carpenters were building a rough-hewn casket made of oak or pine. There were usually men in the neighborhood who were designated for this grim task because they were especially skilled in carpentry. The men of the community and church also took it upon themselves to hand dig the grave with a pick and shovel, which usually proved to be grueling and backbreaking work thanks to compacted clay and rocky soil.

Speaking of graves, before there were so many churches in the area with burial grounds, families commonly laid their loved ones to rest in family plots near the home. One may still run across one of these family cemeteries quite unexpectedly while wandering out in the woods or close to an old, abandoned homeplace. In recent years, there have frequently been reports of large construction projects coming to a grinding halt because workers inadvertently excavated a long-forgotten grave that was part of a larger burial ground. Just off State Highway 101 north, not far from the historic Gilreath Mill, there is a large family/community cemetery located on private property. The landowner, though not personally connected to any of the original families buried there, has done a superb job of maintaining his "backyard graveyard." The ancient grave markers in the cemetery are merely worn and weathered fieldstones placed in neat rows. The only recognizable grave among the twenty-two counted there is the plot of Charles Bruce, patriarch of most Greenville County Bruces. And the only reason this grave is identifiable is because it is marked by a modern granite monument that was donated and placed there by the Bruce family. Bruce, a veteran of the American Revolution, may very well have been the first buried here. An early Howard family cemetery, which bears the remains of Captain Thomas Howard, the hero of the Battle of Round Mountain, is located on private land just off State Highway 101 north in northern Greenville County. Howard's burial place is also marked by a relatively new granite monument that was donated in recent years by members of the Howard family.

Gravestone of Captain Thomas Howard. *Courtesy of Ralph Howard.*

Most of the churches of the Dark Corner do have burial grounds adjacent to their buildings. Once again, many of the earliest graves in these churchyards were marked with bare rocks, which were often moved over time, making it virtually impossible to identify the earliest graves. In addition, it was not at all uncommon for slaves to be buried in these older church cemeteries, albeit in a separate section from those who had enslaved them. Segregated in life and segregated in death. These graves were certainly never marked with anything other than a rock, if marked at all. And should these stones be moved, these graves were surely lost forever because slave burials were seldom recorded in church records. The cemetery at Pleasant Grove Baptist Church in Greer dates back at least to the church's founding in 1833. Longstanding and reliable tradition holds that this cemetery contains the remains of many who were once enslaved.

The practice of embalming the dead is an ancient one that extends at least back to the time of the Egyptian pharaohs. The remains of pharaohs are remarkably well preserved to this day due to the rather sophisticated process of mummification. In America, especially in the rural sections of the country, embalming the dead did not become a common practice until after the Civil War. During and immediately after the war, undertakers, as they were then called, went to the battlefields and embalmed the remains of fallen soldiers so their families could return them home to their final resting places. This practice was not widespread, but it was common enough for people, following the Civil War, to gain more of an interest in and more of an appreciation for the art and skills of the embalmer.

The first commercial undertakers in the area of the Dark Corner were the Wood Mortuary of Greer and the Petty Funeral Home in Landrum. Both firms have long and much appreciated relationships with the people of the upper part of Greenville County. The Wood Mortuary is the oldest continuing commercial enterprise in Greer, its founding dating to 1902. Cousins John D. Wood and Terry Wood went into business together selling dry goods and hardware. They also kept a supply of caskets on hand in their store. The caskets must have been a popular item, because in 1925, John D. Wood wisely decided to devote his time to the burgeoning funeral business. He began, in addition to selling caskets, to offer a wide array of funeral services. And for over 120 years, the Wood Mortuary has served area families and remains a family-based operation. Richard H. Wood Jr., John D. Wood's grandson, leads the business today and has succeeded in offering the same level of compassion and care his grandfather offered over a century ago.

Mr. Wood recently reminisced about the variety of services the mortuary has offered down through the years, including an ambulance service that Wood provided all the way up to 1958.

Only able to offer the most basic level of care because the ambulance drivers were morticians, not EMTs, the ambulance/hearse, Wood reflected, was dispatched to the Dark Corner to transport victims of heart attacks and

Right: John D. Wood, founder of Wood Mortuary. *Courtesy of Wood Mortuary*.

Below: Early hearse horses owned by Wood Mortuary. *Courtesy of Wood Mortuary*.

strokes, and sometimes, knife and gunshot wounds to the old Spartanburg General or Greenville General Hospitals.

Also in those early days, Mr. Wood recalled, families would request that the bodies of their departed loved ones, after necessary preparations, be brought back to the home to lie in state until the day of burial. An old and common practice throughout the South back in those days was for family members or neighbors to stay up all night holding a vigil over the deceased. This custom, for the most part, stopped years ago, though occasionally there are still families who request it, and the mortuary gladly complies.

Soon after John D. Wood established his business, he began offering a wide array of services, including embalming and the addition of a horse-drawn hearse. Wood took pride in the stable of well-trained and well-bred horses, noted for their beauty and elegance as they carried Wood's elaborate, windowed black hearse. Customarily, black horses were used for funerals of men, and white horses were used for funerals of women. But families did not always choose to use the hearse. The author well remembers beloved and longtime Wood employee John Oliver Kendrick, who began working for John D. Wood in 1921. He recalled to me his participation in the funeral of Holland Howard, the revenuer who was killed at the foot of Hogback Mountain on January 31, 1924, the subject of chapter 6 of this book. The Howard family chose to forgo the Wood hearse in favor of a two-horse farm wagon to carry Holland Howard's casket from the Howard home to Highland Baptist Church. Kendrick drove the wagon, and Howard's son Jim (the author of *Dark Corner Heritage*) rode alongside him. This was a memorable moment in the career of the legendary mortician who so nostalgically recalled it some sixty years later.

Oftentimes in the early days of the undertaker, even the embalming of the deceased took place at home. Wood Mortuary, as well as other funeral homes, used portable embalming devices. Pictured on the following page is the portable embalming table once used by Wood Mortuary. This table, along with the other necessary equipment, was taken to the home to prepare the body for burial.

The funeral business has now evolved to the point where almost all preparation activity takes place at the mortuary. The family now has very little contact with the deceased from the time of death until burial.

The Petty Funeral Home, now located in Landrum, is another local firm that has been trusted over the years by the families of the Dark Corner. Like Wood's, Petty also remains a family operation, now into the fifth generation of the Petty family. Also, like Wood Mortuary, the Pettys started

Portable embalming table used in homes. *Courtesy of Wood Mortuary.*

out as merchants, selling groceries and dry goods in a small general store that was located near Ebenezer-Welcome Baptist Church in the heart of the Dark Corner. This store was owned and operated by the patriarch of the Petty family, John Lawson Petty. He soon brought his son Tolly into the growing family business. The store soon thereafter moved to Gowensville, where it remained for several years. In the meantime, the family recognized the need for offering burial services to the community. They were already selling caskets. Tolly soon abandoned storekeeping and decided to move entirely into the mortuary business. They moved to Landrum and bought a horse-drawn hearse, and then Tolly then sent his son J.L. to embalming school to further learn the trade. Later, after Tolly's passing, J.L. took over the mortuary and brought his sons into the business. J.L.'s son John ran the firm for several years before his own retirement, and now his children are running the day-to-day operation. And they, too, carry on the fine tradition of compassionate care and service that has set Petty's apart from others over the years.

Much has changed in the Dark Corner in a couple of centuries since its settlement, but one thing never has, and never will change, and that's the grim reality and regularity of death and the subsequent and painful process of mourning that so many go through. And still, to this day, families are comforted and ministered to by their neighbors and churches as well as those on the outside who continue to provide a high level of care through the services they offer.

19

THE BLOCK HOUSE

As far as landmarks of the Dark Corner go, there is one that even predates the iconic Poinsett Bridge (1820). And that would be the pre–Revolutionary War Block House, located near Tryon, North Carolina. A couple of disclaimers here. First, it may be a stretch to say the Block House is in the Dark Corner, per se. Its location would certainly be at its northern extreme, at best. Second, very little remains today of the original Block House fort. A modern home was built near the fort's original site years ago using what is believed to be some of its old timbers.

A block house refers to a fort-like structure that was used for defense against an enemy attack. Though they were also often used as private residences, they could quickly become community gathering spots in times of public crisis. They could be easily identified by portholes in the thick walls that would be used as rifle portals.

The beginnings of the Tryon Block House are veiled in mystery. It is believed that the fort was originally constructed sometime around 1756, during the height of the French and Indian War, when there was much unrest among the Native Americans along the frontier. At various times after that, the Block House served as a vital refuge for area settlers during other periods of Cherokee uprisings—especially during the years 1776 and 1777, when Indian depredations were on the increase. During that same period, other frontier forts were built along the Cherokee boundary line, which is now known as the Greenville-Spartanburg County line. These would include Gowen's Fort, just down the Blackstock Road from the Block House, and Wood's Fort, near modern-day Apalache. And also, there was Fort Prince, near modern-day Wellford. The infamous Hannon and Hampton massacres in the spring of 1776 greatly increased tensions and anxiety in the area and made the Block House and its sister forts even more vital for defense.

Historical marker located in Tryon telling the story of the Block House.

It was here at the Block House in 1776 that a youthful Captain Thomas Howard mustered together a contingent of soldiers to follow him and his Cherokee friend Skyuka into a little-known gap in the mountains to fight and utterly defeat a band of Cherokee marauders wreaking havoc on local settlements and planning a surprise attack on the Block House.

After threats of Indian attacks ceased, the Block House was largely ignored and soon fell into a state of general disrepair. And yet because of its strategic location, it soon became a popular gathering spot for farmers from western North Carolina and beyond who were hauling their goods to South Carolina markets. Because the Block House was located adjacent to the heavily traveled Howard Gap Road, it often became a camping place for those passing that way. The Howard Gap Road, named in honor of Captain Thomas Howard, closely followed the routes of modern-day US Highways 176 and 25, meandering through the foothills and mountains from near Asheville, North Carolina, all the way to Spartanburg, South Carolina. Since so many travelers were camping and spending time at the Block House, it became known as a place where a lot of Dark Corner moonshine was being consumed. Gambling and other vices became commonplace as well. The Block House continued to be frequented up to and even after the Civil War.

During the Civil War, the Block House became a notorious refuge for deserters and outliers who then populated the mountains in great numbers. In order to understand this phenomenon, one must be familiar with the history of the Civil War in western North and South Carolina. Many mountaineers were opposed to the war and sympathetic to the Union cause for a variety of reasons. First, there were few slaves in the mountains, and the few who may have been there were the exception rather than the rule. Most crops grown in the mountains and hill country, unlike cotton and rice down east, did not require slave labor. Most mountain farms consisted of just a few acres, unlike the hundreds of acres usually held by Lowcountry planters. As a result, a great number of upcountry farmers and residents could not understand why they should be willing to risk their lives so that a few Lowcountry aristocrats could maintain their slaves and their opulent lifestyles.

The Dark Corner was a hotbed of this kind of pro-Union sentiment. This pro-Union attitude extended back to the days of the Nullification Crisis of 1832 when the residents of the Dark Corner voted overwhelmingly against nullification and possible secession. Their sentiment in favor of the Union remained strong even up to and after the Civil War.

During Reconstruction, Union officer John William DeForest was assigned leadership of the recently founded Freedmen's Bureau in Greenville. After the war, he wrote his memoir, titled, *A Union Officer in the Reconstruction*. He wrote about his admiration for the loyal mountaineers of the Dark Corner. DeForest spoke of one incident in particular that displayed the loyalty of the Dark Corner residents for the Union cause. He said,

> *It is a striking instance of the reliability of history that I never learned to my satisfaction the date or manner of the famous advance of the mountaineers upon Greenville during the war. One informant assured me that it took place before Bull Run; that the loyal men of the Dark Corner and vicinity mustered six hundred strong; that they marched toward the low country with the intention of forcing South Carolina back into the Union.*[52]

Outliers and deserters were usually men who either avoided the Confederate draft altogether or deserted from the Confederate army after having been conscripted into service. Many of those outliers found in the mountains were men of the Dark Corner who were evading service, and this number also included a few Union soldiers who had escaped Confederate prison camps and were attempting to make it back to the Union lines.

The rugged Blue Ridge mountains were the perfect refuge for these outliers and deserters, and evidently the old Block House near Tryon became one of these gathering places for this group of desperate refugees.

Mann Batson relates in his book *A History of the Upper Part of Greenville County, S.C.* an episode that took place during the Civil War between officials of the Confederate government and a group of deserters holed up at the Block House. He recalled, "A group of well-organized outliers took possession of the Block House near the State line putting up strong resistance against the authorities. They were so well fortified that Major Ashmore requisitioned a

The Cherokee Rock marking the location of the beginning of the Cherokee boundary line, as well as the North Carolina and South Carolina line. Located near the Block House.

cannon to be used by his men to bring them under control."[53] The men did finally surrender after being threatened with a cannon barrage.

The Block House and the area surrounding it also served as an important geographical boundary marker. After Governor Glen's treaty with the Cherokee in 1755, a boundary was set; it follows the modern-day Greenville-Spartanburg County line, beginning at the state line near the Block House and proceeding south toward the Reedy River. North of the Block House, the boundary line extended all the way to Virginia. All land west of the line belonged to the Cherokee, and all the land east of the line belonged to the State of South Carolina. A triangular stone that can still be seen in a pasture near the site of the old Block House is called the Cherokee Stone, and it marks the old Indian boundary line as well as the spot where North and South Carolina meet.

The Block House remained virtually in ruins for years until 1942, when its remnants were purchased and used to build a modern home. The home still stands today, after having gone through several renovations over the years. It still stands close to the original site of its 1756 construction.

Aside from the weathered historical markers used to tell the story of the Block House, the only other reminder that it ever existed is a wildly popular steeplechase race held annually that bears its name. Newer generations, though, need to be reminded of the proud and important history of this iconic Dark Corner landmark.

20

DARK CORNER MEDICINE

Settlers on the American frontier in the eighteenth and early nineteenth centuries faced any number of natural calamities that could have significantly shortened their lives. In addition to Indian attacks, wild animal attacks and dearth leading to malnutrition and starvation, there was also a wide range of physical maladies that could strike and prove to be fatal. Of course, in those earliest days, medical care was, for the most part, nonexistent. In the first place, medical science was really in its infancy, and what little knowledge people did have was typically limited to the larger cities along the Eastern Seaboard, pretty much leaving isolated mountain communities to their own devices.

Some of the potential medical disasters facing frontiersmen back then included epidemics of fatal communicable diseases like smallpox that could easily and quickly spread from one family member to another and then from one family to another. Soon entire communities would be stricken. Mosquito-borne illnesses were not nearly as common in the upcountry as they were in the Lowcountry. In fact, mountain communities like Flat Rock, North Carolina, were developed and seasonally populated by wealthy Lowcountry planters who brought their families there in the summer to escape the heat and the mosquito infestations that spawned illnesses like yellow fever and malaria. And yet these diseases were not totally unknown in upcountry settlements. Another potentially deadly disease common on the frontier was a malady known as milk sickness. It is believed that milk sickness was caused by drinking milk from a cow that had been feeding on an especially toxic root. Severe sickness and even death would often result. Abraham Lincoln's mother died from milk sickness. And then there were a variety of deadly illnesses that could be caused by drinking from contaminated water sources. Cholera, typhoid and even polio were potentially transmitted through drinking from wells or streams that might have been contaminated with these deadly organisms. This was a time in history when even a drink of water could kill you! All this plus the threat of pneumonia, ruptured appendices and the hazards of childbirth. It was a dangerous world, and it's no wonder life expectancy in the Dark Corner was considerably lower than it is today.

So, what exactly did Dark Corner medical care look like in the early to mid-1800s? Suffice it to say it was primitive at best. European immigrants brought with them what little curative knowledge and understanding they had acquired over time. Medical care in those days consisted mainly of compounds of roots, herbs and tree bark. Coming to America, they discovered that in so many ways they had to start all over again because they were encountering some new and completely unknown botanical species.

Overwhelmed by their new surroundings, they began to turn to their Native American neighbors for advice. These Indigenous peoples, over the vast centuries of their residency here, had become especially adept at using the available natural resources to their own advantage. One noted Cherokee authority described this epochal process:

> *There can be no doubt that in the course of time a haphazard use of plants would naturally lead to the discovery that certain herbs are efficacious in certain combinations of symptoms. These plants would thus come into more frequent use and finally would obtain general recognition in the Indian materia medica.*[54]

As white settlers and the Cherokee came to friendlier terms prior to the Cherokee removal in 1836, the settlers were able to learn much from their Native American neighbors about survival in the wilderness, and this included, no doubt, lessons about curing and preventing illnesses using Cherokee methods, herbs, roots and tree bark, along with other naturally growing plants found in forest and field.

Also, over time, the frontiersmen made important discoveries on their own that had medical value. Some examples of these natural remedies included things like the use of spiderwebs to stop a wound from bleeding. It worked! But who knew in 1820 that it did work because spiderwebs contain high levels of Vitamin K, which promotes blood clotting? Every

Pipsisewa. A plant that grows naturally in the woodlands of the Dark Corner and has been used for generations by Native Americans and white settlers as a cure for kidney stones and bladder issues.

spring, the intrepid Dark Corner residents would take to the woods to gather leaves, plants and roots to concoct teas and tonics they wholeheartedly believed would build their blood and promote natural immunities. They swore by a tea brewed from the leaves of the wild cherry tree, which grew in abundance in the forests of the Dark Corner. Another highly sought-after tonic was made from the fragile and lovely lady's slipper, a wildflower found growing in marshy ground near creeks. The duration of the common cold was believed to be significantly shortened by a tea made from boneset. Even boiled pine needles were thought to cure a cold.[55]

And of course, any discussion of Dark Corner folk medicine would be incomplete without talking about the legendary madstone. Dean Campbell discusses the tradition surrounding the madstone in his book *Eyes to the Hills*. He explained,

> *Madstones have been called by many names. Handed down from generation to generation, these hard, stone-like growths were taken from the head, stomach or bladder of a deer, which had eaten leaves from a tree said to be poisonous to other animals. They were used to draw poison from bites of rabid animals, or poisonous snakes and spiders. The porous stones were washed in warm water or milk and placed on the rabid bite area, which had been pricked in order to draw blood. If the bite contained poison, the madstone stuck to the flesh, turning loose when all the poison was drawn out. Once loosened, the madstone was placed back into warm milk. Small, greenish streaks would emanate from the madstone as poison left its pores. One medical doctor in the Dark corner made occasional use*

> *of a madstone openly, while others were said to use them secretively on a number of occasions.*[56]

Dean Campbell then told the story of Furman Sudduth, a Dark Corner native who carried a madstone with him almost every day of his life and swore by its magical and mysterious properties.

Early on, up in the Dark Corner and other backcountry communities, before local, trained physicians were common, there was customarily one person in the community people looked up to for medical care. Typically, this person was an older woman known as the "yarb doctor," *yarb* being an old mountain term for "herb." We might call them herbalists today. Their knowledge of using herbs and other natural resources for healing exceeded the knowledge of others in the community. This "Granny," as she would

Furman Sudduth's madstone. *Photo from* Eyes to the Hills, *by Dean Campbell. Used by permission.*

sometimes be called, might have an extensive herb garden growing close by to her humble cabin. And she also had a well-worn path out into the woods where she knew the exact location of carefully guarded roots and berries. There she may have a secret patch of the magical ginseng root. She was well familiar with the ingredients, from which she could easily concoct any variety of teas, tonic and poultices. Still today there are those old folks who swear by yellow poot, a potent, light-colored root that grows by upcountry creek banks, and reportedly creates a tea, that if taken in the springtime, produces powerful results. In fact, up until recently, yellow root was sold in the produce department of a local grocery store.

And so, for many years this was pretty much the extent of medical care available in the Dark Corner and, in fact, most rural communities around America. After the Civil War, and into the early twentieth century, clinically trained physicians began practicing their craft on a much wider scale. While medical training and education in those early days was nothing compared to what it is now, it was so much better than what had been available before. Medical schools in Europe were just beginning to share the critical discoveries modern science, just in its infancy, was making. Also, as a result of the bloodshed and carnage of the Civil War, field doctors were making on-the-job discoveries about the human body in real time. And in the process, they were honing their medical skills under the most horrendous of circumstances.

As a result of all this, there were a few trained physicians in place in and around the Dark Corner who were offering their limited services. Since little cash was on hand in those days, doctors were sometimes paid (if they were paid at all) with produce from the field and garden, chickens, eggs and, sometimes, even Dark Corner whiskey. Few would be turned away by these dedicated and compassionate country doctors. They worked tirelessly. They made house calls throughout the community and were known to sit up all night with sick patients and expectant mothers. Their in-home offices were furnished sparsely with only the most basic medical equipment. And sometimes they had offices that were detached from their homes and were little more than small outbuildings where they could examine patients who came to them. This would give the patient a measure of privacy and a place where the doctor could dispense what little treatment and medication he might have. The country doctor, along with the country preacher, was one of the most admired and respected members of the community.

A couple of these Dark Corner physicians worth noting include, first, a bachelor country doctor who practiced in the community in the early years of the twentieth century. His name was Dr. John A. Lindsey, and he was born in 1865 and died in 1924. A devout Christian and churchman, Dr. Lindsey was a member of Glassy Mountain Baptist Church for many years. He was never married, and he owned no home of his own. For several years, he boarded with the Wilson family at Highland. The Wilsons lived in the old Lewis H. Dickey plantation home at the intersection of State Highways 414 and 101. It's unknown what the relationship might have been between Lindsey and the Wilsons, whether family or just friends. Nevertheless, he made his home with them for several years. He also maintained a small office not far behind the main house. It was known in the community simply as the "Doctor's Shop," and it stood for many years until it was finally razed at about the same time as the old main house. Lindsey was much beloved in the community and spent a lot of his time traveling from home to home, but he kept regular office hours on Sunday afternoons. Patients from as far away as Saluda, North Carolina, traveled by buggy or horseback to wait in line to see Dr. Lindsey.[57]

One of the earliest physicians to practice in the Dark Corner was the beloved Dr. William A. Mooney. Mooney was born in 1818 and graduated from the South Carolina Medical College in 1842. He lived and practiced medicine in and around Gowensville. It was there he died at the age of ninety-five. He and his wife are buried at Gowensville Baptist Church, where he faithfully served and attended. Dr. Mooney was present the day of the infamous Mountain Hill Baptist Church shootout on August 23, 1891. He tended to the wounded and dying that day and testified at the coroner's inquest. His son, J. Alender Mooney, was the defense attorney for the accused gunmen.[58]

One more of the great Dark Corner physicians who needs to be mentioned is Dr. Thomas A. Morrow. Dr. Morrow practiced widely throughout the area. His services were sought after as far away as Greer. Morrow graduated from medical school at the University of Tennessee and soon thereafter set up practice in a small office adjacent to his large, attractive Victorian home, which, by the way, is still standing and has been beautifully refurbished. It is located on Morrow Road, just off Highway 14, not far from Gowensville.

Morrow practiced for over fifty years in the area and was much trusted and well loved by the people of the Dark Corner. Dr. Morrow was known to be good at what he did, but there were a couple of stories I heard over the years from locals that reveal the humorous and human side of the old country doctor. It was reputed that Dr. Morrow had named all his rooms in his spacious home after the U.S. states. Now there can be no doubt the kindly

The home of Dark Corner physician Dr. Thomas Morrow.

old doctor worked tirelessly throughout the community, but he, like everyone else, occasionally needed a rest. So, if someone came to his home after hours for help, the doctor was known to send his wife to answer the door while he remained in his bed in a bedroom he had conveniently named "North Carolina" or maybe "Georgia." Thus, his wife might tell the midnight caller,

"I'm sorry, Dr. Morrow is in Georgia tonight." And with this little ploy the fatigued doctor could remain in his warm bed for the evening. At least, that's the story I heard from the old-timers forty years ago.

Also, another anecdote I was told personally regarded Dr. Morrow's "pharmacy." Most of the doctor's prescribed medications consisted of powders wrapped tightly in thin white papers. He kept a supply of these in his coat pocket, and it seems, whatever the ailment, he "prescribed" the same medicine that came out of the same pocket, wrapped in the same white papers. That's certainly not to take away from his skills and abilities. Evidently, he was a very capable physician, considering the level of training and knowledge available back in those days. I heard another personal story about this. A gentleman who lived in Greer had living with him his elderly mother who was bent nearly double with arthritis. She was also in constant pain and distress. The son of this woman had heard that Dr. Morrow was especially proficient at treating arthritic patients, so he went up to the Dark Corner to solicit the old doctor's assistance. Dr. Morrow, well-advanced in years himself, agreed to travel to Greer to this man's home to examine his mother. He prescribed some treatments and medication, no doubt, from his "out of pocket" pharmacy, and after a few such visits, the man told me his mother was remarkably much improved and was able to walk again with some normalcy. Her posture improved as well.

Dr. Morrow continued to practice medicine for many years and died on September 1, 1940. He and his wife are buried at Ebenezer-Welcome Baptist Church.

Fortunately for us, over time, area medical care has improved dramatically. Gone are the kindly country doctors, though, who made house calls and spent time with their patients. Today's highly trained physicians will be found in city clinics, usually working under contract with one of the major hospital systems. While some may nostalgically long for the days of the folksy family physician, we can be very thankful for modern technology that has given us state-of-the-art medical care, drastically improved our quality of life and lengthened our days.

21

DARK CORNER FUN

Hard work with grueling regularity was the normal way of life in the Dark Corner for so many years. There was just no taking a vacation from the daily grind of farming chores. Cows had to be milked twice a day, chickens and hogs had to be fed and fields and gardens had to be tended unless you wanted them taken over by weeds almost overnight. Of course, there was the weekly break for worship on Sundays, but the cows still had to be milked and the chickens and hogs had to be fed. They had no idea it was the Lord's Day. Country folks, just like everyone else, had to take and make time for fun and recreation whenever they could, and they did. And most of the time they practiced great creativity in coming up with ways to have fun.

Community gatherings with close neighbors and friends were always welcome diversions. And when you could combine fun with work that made it all that much better. Community corn shuckings were one good example of this. As we learned earlier, corn was the main crop of Dark Corner farmers. It grew well in just about any soil and thrived with proper cultivation. Survival in the country would have been difficult without it. Corn ground to fine meal was the main ingredient of the much-loved cornbread that often graced the table three times a day. Folks ate it daily with their main meals, and often in the evening a cake of piping-hot cornbread, or cold, crumbled up in a glass of ice-cold sweet milk or buttermilk was enough to hold a body over till breakfast. Corn was also ground for animal feed. And who didn't love a roasting ear or two dredged with freshly churned country butter? It was powerful good eating! Also, admittedly, corn whiskey just couldn't be made without corn. There would be no distilling without it. The corn harvest was greeted each year up in the Dark Corner with the same kind of enthusiasm that it was with the Cherokee.

Typically, a large harvest of corn would be far too much for an individual or even a family to shuck, so the community would be called together for the task. Saturday nights were perfect for corn shuckings. The host family would prepare a large, sumptuous meal that would often be supplemented by desserts or steaming platters others brought in. The host also provided a large, sturdy table made of wooden planks and placed on sawhorses. It would be groaning with delicious offerings soon to be enjoyed by all. Local musicians would brought their instruments and tuned them up to play old familiar mountain ballads during the meal and the shucking activities.

The center of attention, though, was the huge pile of corn stacked in the middle of the barn floor or out in the barnyard, unshucked and ready for busy hands to do the deed. After the meal was over, participants took their place around the pile of corn and began busily shucking, and the corn shucks flew everywhere! Even shucks could be used in the country. Sometimes, in the absence of feathers, they filled beds. Corn shuck dolls were common, and hats were even crafted from corn shucks. As an extra added incentive for the menfolk, the host sometimes included a gallon of Dark Corner "corn-squeezins" at the bottom of the pile. Whoever shucked his way to the bottom first was rewarded with the jug. He was usually kind enough to share it with others. Sometimes, though, things got out of hand because of the available whiskey, and rowdies were called out at the next meeting of the church to give an account for their errant behavior. One such episode of unseemly behavior is recorded in the minutes of Washington Baptist Church, sometime in the 1820s. A brother by the name of John J. Reynolds was called before the elders of the church because he was accused of "Patting juba at a corn shucking for a negro to dance." He was pardoned for his indiscretion. Customarily, though, corn shuckings were pretty sedate events. These kinds of public affairs were also great opportunities for young couples to court. Many a Dark Corner marriage in those early days resulted from corn shucking or candy pulling courtships. And best of all, before the night was over, one happy farmer had most, if not all, of his corn shucked and ready to take to the mill.

Other leisure activities included hunting and fishing, which was a great way for a busy farmer to take a break from his activity to go to the field or stream and, in the process, provide some meat for the table. Thanksgiving Day was the day both quail season and rabbit season opened in most southern states. While the women were usually confined to the kitchen preparing the Thanksgiving feast, the men met up early with shotguns and dogs to take to the field. Rabbit hunting was typically the order of the day on Thanksgiving. And if they started early enough and had some good luck, there might even be some fried rabbit and gravy on the Thanksgiving table along with the turkey and dressing. Quail season lasted until March. Good bird dogs, pointers and setters, were prized by Dark Corner sportsmen, and it wasn't at all unusual after the daily chores were done for the farmer to take to the field with his dogs to find a covey or two with what little sunlight he might have left. What fishing was done locally would have to be done, perhaps, in a farm or millpond or, maybe, in a creek or river, but it was usually slim pickings for the Dark Corner angler, perhaps a catfish or a bony horny head.

Later baseball and softball found their way to the Dark Corner. Baseball games were generally pick-up games and might be held in a field or pasture. Few recreational leagues existed early on, but later, with improved transportation, Dark Corner youth could join teams in Greer, Landrum or Travelers Rest. Church softball came later, and there were teams for men and women. The women were as competitive as the men, and games were always interesting. Just outside the Dark Corner and south on Highway 14, a well-kept softball field known as Gibson Field accommodated church ball teams and church leagues throughout the northern part of the county. Gibson Field was the brainchild of Darwin Gibson, who owned the land where the field was located and lived close by. The field operated for years and was the site of some heated contests. Fans of both teams sat on a bank beside the field and cheered their team on and sometimes jeered at the opposing teams and fans. It made for some interesting evenings.

There's no way one can speak of good times and leisure activities in the Dark Corner or any other rural community without mentioning the role music played in it all. Mountain people throughout the Blue Ridge and Appalachians and beyond were musical people. This was, of course, by personal preference, but you could also make an argument to say it was in their blood and deeply ingrained in their personality. This rich heritage of love for music did not just originate in the hills and hollers of the Carolina and Tennessee mountains. It was brought there by their ancestors from the shires and countryside of England, from the moors and green dales of Ireland and from the highlands of Scotland. Of course, lonely isolation in the mountains only heightened and seasoned the desire to resin a fiddle bow or string up an old open-backed banjo. It is a fact that the fiddle or the banjo played with a certain tone bears a haunting resemblance to the sound made by a Celtic bagpipe. And this music just naturally sets these descendants of the British Isles to dancing a merry jig.

And although these merry jigs may have been frowned on by the straitlaced Baptist preachers of the frontier, it didn't prevent the frequent break out of lively clogging and square dancing. Both styles of dance required exacting precision along with impeccable timing and rhythm. To this day, several mountain colleges and universities raise mountain dance teams to compete against each other. Clogging scholarships are even available for skilled dancers who want to continue their college educations.

The Dark Corner was no different than any other mountain community when it came to a love for old-time music. Many were accomplished musicians and played every chance they got. Playing music, especially after a busy day in the fields, was a welcome diversion around the fire in the evenings. And there were families well-known in the Dark Corner for their musical abilities. The Barnettes were one such musical family whose homeplace was close to Ebenezer-Welcome Baptist Church. Carolyn Chisam was a member of this musical clan and reminisced recently about all the cherished memories she accumulated over the years of gatherings with cousins and aunts, uncles and grandparents on Saturday nights to play the old tunes. Her father, the late Carl Barnette, was a multitalented Dark Corner musician who mastered both the guitar and the banjo. Carolyn spoke nostalgically of the memories she has of sitting in her father's lap while he picked the old-time banjo or strummed the guitar. Carolyn still treasures those memories and recalls how the room would ring with strains of "Old Joe Clark," "Black-Eyed Susie" and "Sourwood Mountain." So many of the songs the hill people sang and played were the same ones their ancestors brought with them from the old country, with slight variations. Sometimes it was the ancient tune with new lyrics and then sometimes the old lyrics with a new tune. And many of those songs reached all the way back to Elizabethan times. "Barbara Allen" was a gut-wrenching ballad commonly played in the mountains, but it could be traced back across the Atlantic to England, where it originated in the 1600s. "Barbara Allen" shared a trait with many of the old mountain ballads, which were so often sad, tragic tales of unrequited love and murder. Music historians tell us many of these ancient "murder ballads" were actually based on true stories, and the more mournful and gory it got, the more popular it seemed to be.

Naturally, over time so many of these old tunes were lost as generations passed off the scene. And as America entered the twentieth century, the old ballads continued to lose favor with the young people, who were, at that

Bacom Lamar Lunsford with the banjo. *Courtesy of the Bascom Lamar Lunsford Scrapbook, Southern Appalachian Archives, Mars Hill University.*

time, enamored of jazz and the new country music that first came out of Bristol, Virginia, with Jimmie Rodgers and the Carter Family. A little later, the center of the country music universe moved to Nashville, Tennessee, and the Grand Ole Opry became the premier Saturday night event on the radio. One native of the mountains refused to let the old songs and ballads fade away. He was a resident of the South Turkey Creek community in Buncombe County, North Carolina, and his name was Bascom Lamar Lunsford, well-known as the "Minstrel of the Appalachians." Lunsford was a lawyer by trade, maintaining a law office in Asheville, but he spent much of his time traveling from one mountain community to the other throughout the Appalachians collecting traditional mountain folk songs and ballads, which were quickly disappearing from the American musical landscape. Lunsford literally went about collecting hundreds of these ancient tunes, carefully writing down lyrics, tunes and where and when he gathered them. In 1927, Lunsford singlehandedly organized the world-famous Mountain Dance and Folk Festival in Asheville, North Carolina, which showcased mountain talent and especially highlighted the old music, which was the rich tradition of the hills. This event became an annual affair that continues to this day. Lunsford, who died in 1973 at the age of ninety-one, is still revered in circles of traditional music. Mars Hill University houses the Bascom Lamar Lunsford Collection, which includes his journals, newspaper articles related to his work, posters and flyers advertising his festivals and even a collection of his musical instruments. It's a shrine, of sorts, for anyone fascinated by the old music of the mountains.

Interestingly, there is a record of Lunsford traveling down into the Dark Corner on one of these music gathering expeditions. He recorded the following entry in his journal in 1927. He noted that he collected an old song called, "'John Kirby' (about a Dark Corners' killing). Mrs. Etta McKinney, Tigerville in the Dark Corners (between North and South Carolina)."[59] Sometime ago, while wandering through the cemetery of Highland Baptist Church, I happened upon the grave of Mrs. Etta McKinney, and I remembered her role in assisting Bascom Lamar Lunsford in his collection of the old songs. Bascom Lamar Lunsford's legacy lives on. Anyone interested in further studying the life story of this fascinating and determined man should read Loyal Jones's biography of Lunsford titled *Minstrel of the Appalachians*.

Sacred music has long been an important part of Dark Corner life. On many a Sunday evening after church, Dark Corner family and friends came together in someone's home and circled around an old upright piano, barely in tune, or an ancient pump organ, and sang one song after another from tattered hymnals and well-worn and well-used paperback editions of Stamps-Baxter songbooks. Many of these books were shaped note songbooks purchased at "singing schools" and conventions, once so popular across the South.

The tradition of old-time gospel singing schools goes back at least to the early 1800s. William Walker was one of its earliest proponents. Born in Union County, South Carolina, in 1809, Walker soon earned the nickname "Singing Billy" from his friends and family. As a pioneer in the old, so-called fa-so-la style of music training, Walker held singing schools throughout the South, training a whole generation of southerners to sing gospel tunes using shaped notes, each note representing a different tune on the musical scale. William Walker is credited with publishing one of the most popular and historically significant hymnals of all time. His 1835 publication of *Southern Harmony* introduced singers to some of the older as well as relatively newer gospel songs. One such hymn was the much-loved "Amazing Grace," which began its life in relative obscurity. Penned by a former slave trader become Anglican priest, John Newton, the song began as a poem with the rather nondescript title "Faith's Review and Expectation." A little later someone set it to music, but again, the tune, like the title, did the great poem little justice. William Walker rediscovered the poem, rescued it from obscurity, gave it the new title "Amazing Grace" and set it to a new, unforgettable tune that came from an old British song called "New Brittain." After this, its popularity skyrocketed when it was included in Walker's new publication *Southern Harmony*.

An interesting side note on William Walker. Walker was conducting one of his singing schools in the Dark Corner at Crossroads Baptist Church, which was located at that time about a mile west of Gowensville. It was probably 1846, and Walker was surprised that such a thriving and growing congregation was worshiping in such cramped conditions. He told them they could do better. It so happened that William Walker owned land in Gowensville, and so, in an act of great Christian generosity, he gifted the church with about five acres of prime real estate on a beautiful hillside with a commanding view of the mountains, just north of Gowensville. In 1848, the church moved to the new site and remained Crossroads Baptist Church until 1873, when they took the name Gowensville Baptist church, and it remains in the very same location that "Singing Billy" Walker donated so many years ago. By the way, when Walker signed the deed over to the church, he signed his name "William Walker, A.S.H." A.S.H. stood for "Author Southern Harmony."

Today, many current residents of the Dark Corner are entertained in ways their ancestors could never have dreamed or imagined. Still, there are those remaining who love the old styles of secular and sacred music. Several of the Dark Corner churches still host gospel singings, and there are bluegrass concerts and festivals that frequently pop up here and there. Dark Corner folks still believe in having fun and entertaining and being entertained.

NOTES

Introduction

1. McCuen, *Including a Pile*, 305.
2. Batson, *History of the Upper Part*, 459.

1. A Tale of Two Bridges

3. Batson, *Early Travel*, 3.
4. Batson, *History of the Upper Part*, 54.
5. Batson, *Early Travel*, 3.
6. Campbell, *Rest of Dark Corner's Twice-Told Tales*, 66.
7. Batson, *History of the Upper Part*, 53.
8. Campbell, *Rest of Dark Corner's Twice-Told Tales*, 67.

2. On Top of Old Hogback

9. Batson, *History of the Upper Part*, 74.
10. Stehlik, *Distilling the Mysteries*, 159.
11. Ibid., 26.

3. *A Story of True Friendship*

12. Ibid., 25.

4. *A Mountain Boy's Life Story*

13. Landrum, *Colonial and Revolutionary History*, 96.
14. Crain, *Mountain Boy's Life Story*, 10.
15. Ibid., 25.
16. Ibid., 6.
17. Westmoreland, *J. Dean Crain*, 139.

5. *Big Alec*

18. Ibid., 144..
19. "Alex Campbell Collapses at End of Quiz by Government's Attorney," *Greenville Piedmont*, April 21, 1937.

6. *The Murder of a Revenuer*

20. "Still Is Breeding Place for Crime. Son of Slain Man Says That Moonshine Still Is Root of Evil," *Greenville News*, February 17, 1924
21. Howard, *Dark Corner Heritage*, 41.

7. *Thunder in the Mountains*

22. Ibid., 86.

8. *A Jail Break to Remember*

23. Campbell, *Rest of Dark Corner's Twice-Told Tales*, 49.
24. Batson, *History of the Upper Part*, 461.

9. *A Tender Farewell*

25. Campbell, *Twice-Told Tales*, 11.
26. Batson, *History of the Upper Part*, 166.
27. Ibid.
28. Batson, *Early Travel*, 3.
29. Edgar, *South Carolina*, 336.
30. Flynn, *Militia in Antebellum South Carolina*, 23.
31. Batson, *History of the Upper Part*, 95.

10. *The Boy from Horse Creek*

32. Ibid.
33. Parris, *Roaming the Mountains*, 79.
34. Ibid., 79.
35. Gilbert, *Trailblazers*, 173.

11. *Grinding Corn in the Dark Corner*

36. Parris, *Roaming the Mountains*, 81.
37. Buttala and Siegel, *Seed Garden*, 342.
38. Batson, *Water-Powered Gristmills*, 3.

12. *The Hensley Burning*

39. Ibid., 144.
40. Howard, *Dark Corner Heritage*, 82.
41. Campbell, *Twice-Told Tales*, 81.

14. *Trouble in a Jug*

42. Batson, *History of the Upper Part*, 471.
43. Howard, *Dark Corner Heritage*, 42.
44. Gilreath, *P.D. Gilreath*, 55.
45. Bledsoe, *Just Folks*, 208.

15. A Dark Corner Hero

46. Ibid., 207.
47. Crain, *Mountain Boy's Life Story*, 26.
48. Minutes of the North Greenville Baptist Association, 1909.

16. Dickey's Plantation

49. Howard, *Dark Corner Heritage*, 62.

17. Shootout at Mountain Hill Church

50. Batson, *History of the Upper Part*, 109.
51. Ibid.

19. The Block House

52. Ibid., 468–69.
53. Morley, *Carolina Mountains*, 73.

20. Dark Corner Medicine

54. DeForest, *Union Officer in the Reconstruction*, 160.
55. Batson, *History of the Upper Part*, 433.
56. Mooney, *History, Myths and Sacred Formulas*, 323.
57. Wigginton, *Foxfire Book*, 231–32.
58. Campbell, *Eyes to the Hills*, 24.

21. Dark Corner Fun

59. Howard, *Dark Corner Heritage*, 75.

BIBLIOGRAPHY

Batson, Mann. *Early Travel and Accommodations.* Taylors, SC: Faith Printing, 1995.

———. *A History of the Upper Part of Greenville County, S.C.* Taylors, SC: Faith Printing, 1993.

———. *Water-Powered Gristmills and Their Owners.* Taylors, SC: Faith Printing, 1996.

Bledsoe, Jerry. *Just Folks.* Charlotte, NC: East Woods Press, 1980.

Buttala, Lee, and Sharyn Siegel. *The Seed Garden.* Decorah, IA: Seed Saver's Exchange, 2015.

Campbell, Dean. *Eyes to the Hills.* Landrum, SC: Tamaczar Productions, 1994.

———. *The Rest of the Twice-Told Tales of the Dark Corner.* Landrum, SC: Tamaczar Productions, 2017.

———. *Twice-Told Tales of the Dark Corner.* Landrum, SC: Tamaczar Productions, 2013.

Crain, J. Dean. *A Mountain Boy's Life Story*. Greenville, SC: Baptist Courier, 1914.

DeForest, John William. *A Union Officer in the Reconstruction*. Baton Rouge: Louisiana State University Press, 1997.

Edgar, Walter. *South Carolina: A History*. Columbia: University of South Carolina Press, 1998.

Flynn, Jean. *The Militia in Antebellum South Carolina Society.* Spartanburg, SC: Reprint Company, 1991.

Gilbert, Bil. *The Trailblazers*. Alexandria, VA: Time-Life Books, 1973.

Gilreath, John H. *P.D. Gilreath, High Sheriff*. Greenville, SC: John H. Gilreath, 1968.

Hines, Drew. *In Mountain Shadows. The Story of Washington Baptist Church, Greer, SC, 1819–2019.* Greenville, SC: Courier Publishing Company, 2019.

Howard, James A. *Dark Corner Heritage*. Landrum, SC: James A. Howard, 1980.

Jones, Loyal. *Minstrel of the Appalachians*. Lexington: University of Kentucky Press, 1984.

Landrum, J.B.O. *Colonial and Revolutionary History of Upper South Carolina*. Spartanburg, SC: Reprint Company, 1977.

McCuen, Anne K. *Including a Pile of Rocks*. Greenville, SC: Southern Historical Press, 2005.

Mooney, James. *History, Myths and Sacred Formulas of the Cherokees*. Fairview, NC: Historical Images, 1992.

Morley, Margaret W. *The Carolina Mountains*. Fairview, NC: Historical Images, 1913.

Parris, John. *Roaming the Mountains*. Asheville, NC: Citizen Times Publishing, 1955.

Stehlik, James. *Distilling the Mysteries of Hogback Mountain.* Landrum, SC: James Stehlik, 2011.

Westmoreland, Lillie B. *J. Dean Crain, A Biography*. Greenville, SC: Hiott Press, 1959.

Wigginton, Eliot. *The Foxfire Book.* New York, NY: Anchor Books, 1972.

INDEX

G

H

J

K

L

M

N

O

P

V

W

Y

ABOUT THE AUTHOR

Drew Hines is a native of Greensboro, North Carolina, but has spent most of his life in the upstate of South Carolina. A Baptist minister for forty-three years, he's now retired and enjoys writing, gardening and traveling. He has been married for forty-seven years to Suzanne, and they have two adult children and five grandchildren. He is a graduate of the University of South Carolina and is the recipient of two postgraduate degrees from the Southern Baptist Theological Seminary in Louisville, Kentucky. He is the author of two other books: *In Mountain Shadows* and *North of Jordan*. He also writes a column on local and regional history for the *Tryon Daily Bulletin* in Tryon, North Carolina.